Robots in Law:
How Artificial Intelligence is Transforming Legal Services

JOANNA GOODMAN

'You just can't differentiate between a robot and the very best of humans'

Isaac Asimov, *I, Robot*

Head of events and books
Leah Darbyshire

Commissioning editor
Laura Slater

Editorial assistant
Edward Bowes

Published by ARK Group:

UK, Europe and Asia office
6–14 Underwood Street
London, N1 7JQ
United Kingdom
Tel: +44(0) 207 566 5792
publishing@ark-group.com

North America office
4408 N. Rockwood Drive, Suite 150
Peoria IL 61614
United States
Tel: +1 (309) 495 2853
publishingna@ark-group.com

www.ark-group.com

Cover image by Sam Mardon, sam@onemanfilm.co.uk

Layout by Susie Bell, www.f-12.co.uk

Printed by Canon (UK) Ltd, Cockshot Hill, Reigate, RH2 8BF, United Kingdom

ISBN: 978-1-78358-264-8

A catalogue record for this book is available from the British Library

ARK Group is a division of Wilmington plc. The company is registered in England &
Wales with company number 2931372 GB. Registered office: 6–14 Underwood Street,
London N1 7JQ. VAT Number: GB 899 3725 51.

Contents

Part 1: Legal AI – Beyond the hype

Part 2: Putting AI to work

Part 3: AI giving back – Return on investment

Part 4: Looking ahead... but not too far!

Foreword

By Richard Tromans, innovation consultant to law firms at TromansConsulting and editor of ArtificialLawyer.com

Artificial intelligence (AI) is no longer a subject for conference debates about the far future. Legal AI is not a matter of 'what if', or even 'when'. It is happening right now. The real question lawyers should be asking themselves is how do they need to respond.

All the more reason then for a book such as this, written by one of the UK's leading technology journalists, Joanna Goodman, which provides a helpful introduction to AI and consideration of where the technology has got to so far.

Joanna sensibly looks at the subject from a practical perspective and considers the direct impact that AI will have on law firms, rather than getting lost in philosophical and futurological debates (as many other books on the subject have done in the past).

A practical approach is the right one because AI is a tool. You don't have to understand how a tool was made to use it. And this is the scenario that many lawyers are in now. That is to say, let's not worry too much about coding and algorithms but instead focus on what legal AI can do for lawyers, in law firms, within in-house teams, and across businesses in general.

When I am discussing innovation and AI with law firm clients, the reality is that although managing partners and general counsel are intrigued by how the technology works, what they really want to know is how to use it. They want to know which types of AI system to use, and where or how to use them.

Law firms also want help with developing solutions for clients that will make the best use of legal AI applications. Because, after all, if there were no real benefit to the clients, legal AI's impact would be limited to internal efficiency gains, and the technology is capable of delivering far more than that.

There are other benefits such as helping to reduce costs, improve associate retention due to the reduction in dull process work, and an increase in productivity. Then there are the 'soft' benefits, such as helping a law firm to build deeper and broader client relationships. While for corporates there is the realisation that legal AI can be tapped not just by the in-house team, but by non-lawyer executives across the company, for example to speed up contract review.

There are so many ways that legal AI can bring positive change to the world of lawyers and legal work. And we have only just started to appreciate how useful it can be. From contract review to expert systems, to case prediction and matter triage, to linking with broader automation systems and creating AI-driven legal research systems, there are myriad uses.

This may all sound very positive. And it is. Using legal AI could provide a type of modern renaissance to the legal sector, reducing the need to do process work and allowing lawyers to focus on what they are best at and have been trained to do: give legal advice.

However, there is now a new challenge. No sooner have we overcome the hype that is associated with any new technology than we are faced with more practical challenges, such as how to use legal AI, how to measure its performance, and how to build models for understanding return on investment.

Every law firm is different, so is every in-house team. That means few lawyers will have exactly the same AI needs. Even where there are similar needs, different practice groups will seek to use certain AI systems in different ways. Certain types of client will also benefit from particular types of application.

As one can appreciate, there is much to think about when it comes to making use of AI in the legal sector. That being the case, Joanna's book is a great starting point that will set readers on the right track by informing them and providing useful groundwork.

After reading this book, law firms and in-house teams will hopefully be in a position to begin the next phase in this new era of legal technology, which will be to develop a new innovation strategy that will embrace AI, decide what types of AI are best for their organisations and staff, and then move to the trialling and implementation phases.

Law schools and technology developers and suppliers reading the book will gain a better understanding of how AI is augmenting and leveraging lawyers' skills and knowledge, improving efficiencies, and transforming the industry.

Introduction

'The future is here, it is just not very evenly distributed.' William Gibson's quote from 2003 is a pretty good description of where artificial intelligence (AI) has got to so far in the legal sector.

The year 2016 is a milestone for legal AI. Enterprise technology has caught up with legal futurists Richard and Daniel Susskind, Chrissie Lightfoot, and others who predicted robot lawyers. A handful of leading law firms and alternative legal services providers have now successfully introduced AI technology into multiple elements of legal services delivery.

Everyone likes robots – or do they? As AI continues its incursion into our lives and work, the legal sector is experiencing the same excitement and fear that we are seeing elsewhere/in the wider world in relation to other aspects of AI – such as driverless or semi-autonomous vehicles and digital assistants.

The fear is not about automation – firms have used workflow technology for many years. The differentiator between automation and AI is machine learning. AI software is trained to fulfil tasks, take decisions, and respond in real time to natural language queries. Like a human, it is capable of learning by doing, using each experience to improve its output in terms of accuracy and performance. Are lawyers comfortable with delegating legal decision-making – currently involving research and processes – to intelligent software? Are they concerned about how their clients will feel about robot lawyers, or 'driverless' or semi-autonomous legal services? Obviously, this will depend on the nature, context, and significance of the work and the type of technology being applied to it.

The first 'robot lawyers' attracted significant press attention. Examples include legal research assistants – RAVN deployed by

Berwin Leighton Paisner in the UK and ROSS by BakerHostetler in the US – as well as customer-facing, AI-powered applications like Joshua Browder's DoNotPay.co.uk – a free online chatbot that handles parking ticket appeals instead of a lawyer. Consequently, the consultants and commentators who just a few months ago had dismissed legal AI as a 'legal IT buzzword' – and the articles featuring it as 'clickbait' – have turned full circle and are now frantically highlighting its potential to 'reinvent' or 'redesign' law.

The general take-up of cloud computing in law firms and elsewhere, plus significant investment in legal AI, is driving the development of efficient, accessible, and increasingly cost-effective technology, and fuelling a dynamic global lawtech start-up economy.

While trailblazers are powering ahead with legal AI, the mainstream legal market is waking up to the potential for innovation to deliver benefits. These include enabling law firms to provide faster, more cost-effective legal services while maintaining their margins, and supporting access to justice through scalable not-for-profit and pro bono services.

And this is where *Robots in Law* comes in. The title was inspired by 'Robots and Lawyers', a event held in June 2016 by the Law Society of England and Wales, which focused on the partnership between man and machine in the context of the law and legal services. As technology has become a key element in how we live and work, touching most aspects of our lives, it needs to be covered by the rules of our society. We need to change how we regulate for our connected world, including legal services. But before we regulate, we need to understand how AI fits into legal services delivery – whether it is a facilitator or whether it will significantly change the legal services business model by shifting the value chain.

Following the success of early legal AI models in terms of speed, efficiency, and cost-effectiveness, law firms and other legal services providers are looking at whether and how legal AI can fit into their business operations. There is some confusion as technology vendors recognise a genuine market opportunity and every new offering is styled as incorporating at least an element of legal AI. Legal AI has become inescapable, so this book is an attempt to provide some clarification around defining legal AI and determining its practical application – now and in the short-term.

Robots in Law is not an attempt at comprehensive coverage of everything that's happening in legal AI. The business environment around lawtech is so dynamic that any such effort would be out of date as soon as it was published! Nor do I have the resources or expertise to conduct in-depth research, although I am including input from academics, technology providers, and law firms.

Rather, the aim here is to offer a snapshot of legal AI in 2016 – how it has evolved, what's happening now, and where it might be going. *Robots in Law* is a primer or a starting point for law firms, law schools, or anyone involved in legal technology who wants to get up to speed on legal AI. It brings together leading thinkers and technologists and examples of successful, practical applications of the technology. It is both a progress report and an opinion piece. I cover AI and cutting-edge technology for several national publications in the UK, and I have sought insights from some of the technologists and practitioners who are leading the way in these fields. Finally, I have included some short-term predictions from some of the best-known legal futurists on the future direction and impact of legal AI.

The title *Robots in Law* is a word play on the in-law relationship in a family. You don't choose your in-laws, but the in-law relationship can represent a significant part of your family dynamic, and it may require some careful handling! Legal AI can underpin the business and drive it forward. It can be essential to market positioning, or a useful add-on. Or it might not fit at all, depending on the size and profile of the business and the work being handled. It has reached the point, however, at which it needs to be a strategic consideration because it may well change the legal services business model, affecting business decisions as well as client and supplier relationships.

The relationship between man and machine in the form of intelligent technology has become inescapable in the legal industry, as it has in numerous other sectors. So the challenge for law firms is to leverage their relationship with technology and make it work for them. My intention in writing this book is to look beyond the hype and promises and provide a useful guide, and some food for thought.

Joanna Goodman, 2016

Executive summary

Although 2016 has been the breakthrough year for artificial intelligence (AI) in legal services in terms of market awareness and significant take-up, legal AI represents evolution rather than revolution. Since the first 'robot lawyers' started receiving mainstream press coverage, many law firms, other legal services providers and law colleges are being asked what they are doing about AI.

Robots in Law aims to provide a starting point in the form of an independent primer for anyone looking to get up to speed on legal AI.

The book is organised in four sections. The first three present an overview, and some analysis, of the current legal AI landscape. Part I: Legal AI – Beyond the hype; Part II: Putting AI to work; and Part III: AI giving back – Return on investment. The final section, Part IV: Looking ahead, includes contributions from AI experts with connections to the legal space, on the prospects for legal AI in the short-term future.

Along with the emergence of NewLaw and the global lawtech start-up phenomenon, AI is part of a new dynamic in legal technology. It is here, and it is here to stay. The question now is whether AI will find its place as a de facto facilitator of legal services delivery, and how the shift in the value chain that it undoubtedly brings will transform the legal business model.

Part I: Legal AI – Beyond the hype
Chapter 1: Defining legal AI
Since AI has been applied successfully to legal practice, and has received a lot of media attention, nearly every new legal technology offering seems to be styling itself as legal AI and

multiple vendors and consultants are offering 'thought leadership' which includes various definitions of what AI means for legal services. Chapter 1 cuts through the hype to identify the capabilities which differentiate legal AI from other legal technology tools and services. It looks at where AI fits into a firm's technology architecture and offers some examples of successful use cases for decision makers to consider.

Chapter 2: From BI to AI

Legal AI involves more than applying mathematical forecasting techniques, including sophisticated algorithms, to real-time data. Chapter 2 looks at the evolution from business intelligence (BI) to artificial intelligence (AI) and how mainstream technology offerings provided a jumping-off point for legal AI – notably the progression from intelligent search, contract automation, and collaboration platforms to natural language processing and scalable machine learning – and continue to underpin AI's integration into law firms' technology architecture.

Part II: Putting AI to work

Chapter 3: Legal research – Virtual assistants

The first robots in law were the virtual assistants that support legal research. These are narrow, or applied, AI as they are applied to particular legal specialisms, processes, and challenges. Chapter 3 presents practical examples of AI-powered virtual assistants currently in use, including RAVN deployed at Berwin Leighton Paisner, ROSS at BakerHostetler, and Kira Systems at Clifford Chance.

Chapter 4: 'Driverless' law – An intelligent platform for legal services

This chapter looks at 'AI as a service' in legal including the first robot lawyers! These reflect the development of AI platforms and conversational commerce in other industry sectors. We consider the concept of 'driverless' law in terms of white-labelled intelligent contract creation, as well as the on-demand AI-powered services that support legal services delivery.

Chapter 5: AI first – Service as software

AI first for legal? Chapter 5 explores the concept of service as software as embodied by Viv – Siri co-creator Dag Kittlaus's virtual assistant that generates software in response to real-time natural language queries. Although legal AI has some way to go in that regard, the logical next step for legal AI trailblazers was to build bespoke AI-powered applications that differentiate their services. We look at examples including Riverview Law's Kim – an intelligent platform for in-house legal services – and Neota Logic's expert platform for customer-facing applications, as well as firms with their own in-house developers creating tailored AI-powered services.

Part III: AI giving back – Return on investment
Chapter 6: AI and lawtech start-ups

Legal AI is being accelerated by growing interest in investing in lawtech. This has helped to create (and is driven by) the thriving global lawtech start-up community, which is supported by investors that include law firms as well as the seed funding and angel funding that helps to get start-ups from concept to delivery – and hopefully to expand into successful businesses. Chapter 6 looks at who is creating, investing in, and supporting emerging AI technologies.

Chapter 7: AI for good

Chapter 7 explores some of the ways in which AI is helping to broaden access to justice by giving those who cannot afford to consult a lawyer, or are unsure whether they need one, a way of accessing legal advice with little or no financial outlay. We look at examples of how this is shifting the legal business model and law firm culture. Is legal AI good for the legal services market? Although there is an argument that 'robots' appear to be replacing lawyers, they are also providing new ways for individuals and businesses to exercise and protect their legal rights, and potentially developing more work opportunities for lawyers.

Chapter 8: AI challenges

Chapter 8 examines some of the key legal AI challenges. These include recognising AI's limitations – what it can and cannot do – as well as some of the practical and ethical considerations. We consider cultural issues around roles and work styles in law firms, as well as challenges to the business model, and look at how some firms and vendors are adopting strategies that are turning challenges into opportunities.

Part IV: Looking ahead… but not too far!
Chapter 9: Legal AI – Creating the future

'The best way to predict the future is to create it', said Abraham Lincoln. Chapter 9 takes a futurist perspective on the likely impact of legal AI on legal services delivery, with contributions from futurists and AI experts who speak and write extensively about legal AI, but are not part of the legal establishment. Legal futurist Chrissie Lightfoot, global futurist and strategist Rohit Talwar, and Robert Woolliams, editor and online community manager at AI Business, highlight some of the issues related to and influences on where legal AI is going next and encourage lawyers, legal services providers – and technologists – to engage in creating the future of law.

Chapter 10: Robot lawyers – A new chapter in legal IT

Legal AI has been described as heralding a 'new chapter' in the legal technology arms race. It will surely replace some roles and create others, and it is already altering legal technology purchasing patterns. Chapter 10 speculates on some of the influencing factors on the future direction of legal AI.

About the author

Joanna Goodman is a freelance journalist, writer, and author. She covers business and technology topics for national publications and blue-chip corporates. She is the IT columnist for the *Law Society Gazette* and writes regular features for *The Guardian* about cutting-edge technology, brands, and media. Her favourite topics include artificial intelligence, robots and chatbots, virtual assistants, connected devices, driverless cars, and virtual and augmented reality – and she's always interested in finding out about technology that's new and different. Her professional life reflects her interests in technology, books, art, and design.

Joanna has written several short films and an independent feature film, *Alfheim's Edge* (2016). She has an MBA in strategic management from Kingston University. Joanna is based in London. She likes films, going to dance classes, and travelling to new destinations.

Acknowledgements

Robots in Law brings together expertise and practical insights into the brave new world of legal AI from a broad selection of its leading players. Artificial intelligence is a fast-moving environment and this is not an attempt to be comprehensive. The idea is to present a snapshot of developments for anyone who wants to get up to speed with legal AI. I hope to bring a slightly different perspective on the topic from other commentators, as my background is in media, not law, and I write about technology from an innovation and branding perspective, as well as covering the legal and business sectors.

I'd like to thank everyone who has contributed to *Robots in Law* – not just ideas and insights, but practical and moral support. Contributors include lawyers and technologists in law firms and legal services providers, and legal technology suppliers, as well AI experts and developers, academics, consultants, futurists, and commentators. I appreciate the legal AI providers who took the time – and patience – to demonstrate their products and explain how they work. There are far too many of you to thank individually – I'd need another chapter just to say thanks, but I am so grateful to everyone who has helped.

As part of my research, I needed to learn more about artificial intelligence generally and for this I am indebted to AI Business for including me in their spectacular AI Summits in London and San Francisco, and to Legal Geek for a ground-breaking lawtech start-up conference and their hackathons, all of which happened while I was planning and writing this book. I have relied on fantastic lawtech media start-up Artificial Lawyer for keeping me up to date with developments in legal AI. Thank you all for the information, introductions, and insights.

Acknowledgements

I'm grateful for creative input: written contributions from Chrissie Lightfoot, Rohit Talwar, and Robert Woolliams, and permissions to reproduce images and other materials.

And I also need to mention the red robot who sits on my desk, a gift from my friends at RAVN and inspiration for Sam Mardon's fabulous cover design. Thank you so much!

This book exists thanks to the inspiration and encouragement of my friend Leah Darbyshire, head of events and books at ARK Group – who came up with the idea in the first place – and my fantastic editor Laura Slater who has provided ideas, feedback, and impeccable copy-editing!

Above all, I'd like to thank my family and friends who have been there for me throughout – for helping, understanding, and putting up with me during the writing of this book!

Joanna Goodman, 2016

Part 1:
Legal AI –
Beyond the hype

Chapter 1:
Defining legal AI

Legal AI is an evolution rather than a revolution. Its foundations can be seen in technology already widely and routinely used by law firms. Examples include sophisticated search technology, the e-discovery software that enables technology assisted review (TAR) and document automation. AI is a hot topic and a popular label for new technology offerings. This chapter attempts to look beyond the hype to provide some clarity. In order to do this, we need to consider the background to legal AI, what it actually does, and the capabilities which differentiate it from the rest of legal technology. These are the factors which underpin the business rationale for law firms and legal services providers to introduce AI. The aim here is to provide decision makers with some clarity around the legal AI landscape. AI is not for every business, but it can make a significant difference.

The progression from intelligent search, contract automation, and collaboration platforms to natural language processing, scalable machine learning, and cognitive computing is enabling law firms and legal technology providers to develop automation from straightforward decision trees to more complex functions, where AI's integration into law firms' technology architecture is reducing human involvement in legal research and due diligence.

Since AI has been applied to legal practice, it has received a lot of media attention and in addition to the new AI products appearing in articles and press releases almost every day, many legal technology vendors are styling their existing offerings as AI, or as including an element of AI. Vendors, consultants, and other 'thought leaders' are publishing commentary and opinion pieces on whether, how, and to what extent they envisage AI disrupting the legal sector, and which roles, if any, will be 'taken by robots'. There is a dedicated legal AI news website featuring the latest legal news and product launches. Reading between the lines of scaremongering, enthusiasm – and marketing – it is clear that legal AI is here to stay!

I should reiterate that this book is not intended to provide comprehensive coverage of the rapidly expanding marketplace in AI-powered technology that is targeting legal services. That is changing so fast, that it makes more sense to look at AI news sites like AI Business[1] and *Artificial Lawyer*,[2] which are updated daily. Rather, this is a vendor-neutral attempt to provide some clarity and direction in a sea of information and opinion which is often biased by commentators' business profiles and agendas. Consultants will highlight the projects and clients they are aligned with and vendors are unlikely to present their competitors as market leaders. Although this and the following sections feature some legal AI trailblazers, these are intended as use cases to illustrate the practical application of AI, rather than as a procurement guide.

What is AI?

It is worth establishing the definition of AI before looking at its application to legal services.

The study of AI was first defined at the Dartmouth Artificial Intelligence (AI) conference in 1956 where Stanford researcher John McCarthy proposed a project 'to find how to make machines use language, form abstractions and concepts, solve kinds of problems now reserved for humans, and improve themselves'.[3] The *Oxford English Dictionary* defines artificial intelligence as: 'The theory and development of computer systems able to perform tasks normally requiring human intelligence, such as visual perception, speech recognition, decision making, and translation between languages'.

The Wikipedia definition of artificial intelligence originates from Richard Bellman, who described AI as '[The automation of] activities that we associate with human thinking, activities such as decision-making, problem solving, learning'.[4] Basically, artificial intelligence is about machines (computer software) doing things that are normally done by people.

AI can also be divided into general (strong) AI, which simulates human reasoning – i.e. it thinks like a human and can be used to build software and systems in real time in response to user requirements – and narrow (weak) AI which applies human-type cognitive reasoning to achieve a particular result, like winning a game of chess – or Go. The practical AI that we interact with in our professional and personal lives is mostly narrow AI – apps that can process natural language and images and make decisions and recommendations based on previous choices and behaviours. Narrow AI replicates different aspects of human reasoning, but only for a specific purpose.

In his white paper 'Artificial Intelligence in Law: The State of Play 2016', Michael Mills, co-founder and chief strategy officer at Neota Logic, defines seven branches of AI:

* Machine learning – Deep learning, supervised learning, unsuper-vised learning;
* Natural language processing – Contract extraction, classification, machine translation, question answer, and text generation;
* Expert systems;
* Vision – Image recognition, machine vision;
* Speech – Speech to text, text to speech;
* Planning; and
* Robotics.

Interestingly, all the attributes in the *Oxford English Dictionary* definition can be found on a smartphone, which goes some way towards explaining why AI is so hot right now. Furthermore, AI technology is evolving very quickly. Mills suggests that lawyers do not need robots or machine vision, but

2016 has seen the first robot lawyers and AI-powered due diligence engines include image recognition and machine vision in order to identify particular aspects of documents (photographs, missing pages etc.).

Why is AI so hot right now?

For some years the legal sector – and legal IT – has been predicting its own future. This is partly a reaction to the changes forced on a traditional and conservative industry by market liberalisation, particularly in the UK and Australia, and partly because of the transformational effects of technology on all businesses, especially in terms of communication and collaboration. Because AI in legal is still relatively limited, its disruptive effects generally remain to be seen, but the industry recognises that it has potential to shift the value chain. So, although it may not change significantly the operational business model for most firms, or for the most part the services they offer their clients, it is likely to affect the pricing model – i.e. what clients are prepared to pay for various (elements of) legal services. This has led to a sharp focus on the potential implications of AI. One of the world's top IT lawyers, Richard Kemp, identified AI as a key part of the legal technology architecture: 'AI is "next gen" enterprise software, alongside cloud, data analytics and mobile.' He and others have anticipated that 'it's only AI until you know what it does, then it's just software'.

The same considerations apply across multiple industries and sectors. Although AI has been an important element of operational processes in manufacturing, energy, and healthcare for many years, it has only recently hit the mainstream. This is because it has become a key component of consumer technology, and our connected world: the digital and mobile economy. Recent research has established that this is due to the confluence of several factors, although it is only possible due to the universal take-up – and accessible pricing – of cloud computing as a platform.

A *ZDNet* article about Leading Edge Forum research indicated that the alignment of three factors is propelling AI into the mainstream.[5] These are:

- Big data and predictive analytics – The ability to capture, anonymise, and analyse large quantities of unstructured data to uncover patterns;

- Advances in deep learning software and parallel processing hardware, which are the two main ingredients of machine learning; and

- The general take-up of cloud computing – Cloud is the catalyst as it has made scalable technologies accessible and affordable. Cloud promotes connectivity – including connected devices that link multiple information repositories and processing engines. AI essentially brings together unlimited, unstructured data, complex scalable analytics, and machine learning. All this requires massive processing power and connectivity.

AI also requires a fourth component, not mentioned in the *ZDNet* article: *natural language processing*. This gives AI-powered applications immediacy and intimacy: the intuitive user interface which has driven the take-up of Apple's Siri and Microsoft's Cortana. You can just talk to it – you don't need to search for what you need in a particular way.

These four qualities are what differentiate AI applications from sophisticated search technologies and automated workflows. It's not just about finding information by searching documents and emails for particular words and phrases – it's about software learning to extract the right information from unstructured data, delivering it in a particular format, and using it to guide, choose – or actually take – a particular course of action. Ultimately, it is about software that creates applications, and applications that create software in response to users' stated and implicit requirements.

This combination of technological advances and the cloud-powered digital economy has also proved to be a catalyst for the adoption of AI in legal.

Research and legal AI

Although AI has only hit the legal market and the press in the past 18 months or so, legal AI in its current form has been the focus of academic research since the 1980s. The first international conference on artificial intelligence and law was held in 1987.

Katie Atkinson, professor of computer science at the University of Liverpool, has been publishing research around applying computational models of argument to law, e-democracy, and agent systems since 2003. Her work entails creating computer programmes that apply particular laws to live cases. These are rules-based engines and, as the law is essentially a set of rules, it would seem a perfect fit for AI. It is interesting that in terms of AI take-up, the legal sector is lagging behind other industries where determining rules and potential outcomes are less clear and more challenging.

Why has legal AI taken so long to hit the mainstream? 'For the first time, AI is starting to deliver on promises that have been made since the 1980s', explains Atkinson. 'And we use it in our everyday lives. Smartphones apply natural language processing to enable us to record messages or ask Siri questions. Although driverless cars are limited to controlled environments, our cars include intelligent capabilities like self-parking.'

Games are the traditional testing ground for AI and the past few years have seen some big breakthroughs. In 1996 Big Blue, IBM's chess-playing computer, beat the then-world chess champion, Garry Kasparov, at chess. In 2011 IBM Watson – a computer system capable of answering natural language questions – won the quiz show *Jeopardy*. And in 2016 Google's AlphaGo programme beat Lee Sedol, the world's top Go player. 'The main breakthrough has been to apply techniques that have been developed in a controlled environment to practical business and legal situations', says Atkinson.

In addition to increased processing power that is also cost-effective, Atkinson observes that the workplace generally is more accepting of automation. She is working with Riverview Law to create applications that automate routine tasks and add reasoning that augment human effort. 'AI may change the nature of work, but at the moment I don't envisage it replacing significant numbers of people although that may change as the technology develops', she adds.

Atkinson's work at Liverpool University includes computational models of argument that could ultimately be used to decide legal cases. This is a development in rules-based models to include value-based arguments, balancing objective and subjective information to reflect value preferences like fairness. 'This is to promote decisions that reflect the values that are upheld in society and enshrined in the law – and change over time', she explains. These raise ethical as well as technical challenges.

Where does AI fit into legal IT?

There are two key drivers of legal IT: content management and practice management.

Content management is about creating and storing legal documents and precedents and correspondence, including information exchange and negotiations.

Practice management covers all the operations that run a legal services business – and includes financial management, operations and HR management, business development and marketing, as well as risk management, compliance, and information security. Practice management systems include business intelligence (BI) features that support work allocation and process efficiency, while client-facing technology, such as collaboration platforms and client relationship management (CRM) systems, help to develop new and repeat business.

Gradually, processes have become automated. Automated workflows and document production support productivity with consistent, efficient, and cost-effective processes and built-in compliance. AI can intuitively bring together processes and content to maximise efficient management and service delivery.

On the content side, the focus is on managing large volumes of data to extract the right information, knowledge, and expertise in order to provide clients with the best advice quickly and cost-effectively. Search is the key content management technology and the e-discovery industry has produced highly sophisticated search technologies that can be considered the springboard for legal AI.

A main strand of legal AI has developed from search, a core legal technology that underpins e-discovery and knowledge management generally. As Oz Benamram, chief knowledge officer at White & Case, observes, the immediate precursors to legal AI are the federated search engines that help lawyers at many firms navigate the large number of documents involved in legal work and search internal and external knowledge resources for information that is relevant to the case they are working on. Sophisticated search applications include contextual search – i.e. results include related information, as well as word strings and synonyms. However, context in this sense is based on meaning and history – i.e. it is rules-based rather than cognitive, so the system doesn't read the documents but finds particular words and phrases that relate to context.

E-discovery software combines predictive coding and an element of machine learning to reduce the time and cost of trawling through massive volumes of data in order to extract relevant evidence in complex litigation. Although it applies elements of natural language processing and machine learning – two key elements of AI engines – it is searching structured data for specific terminology. It is therefore a decision tree that applies the same search criteria, which is established by using sampling techniques, to large volumes of data.

AI brings together document automation with sophisticated search technology as used in e-discovery, but unlike e-discovery software, AI engines actually read the data and consider broader variables around context in order to extract particular information and recommend or take action on it. AI needs to be good at identifying exceptions and referring them back for humans to decide. What happens next depends on the context of the data extracted and the set of instructions applied to it.

The main differentiator is machine learning. So rather than simply applying rules in order to classify content, an AI-powered system learns from previous instructions and interactions with data. So, in time, it accumulates expertise, becoming faster and more accurate, and requires less human involvement. Atkinson explains that the biggest challenge is at the outset – the 'knowledge acquisition bottleneck' or, put simply, getting the requisite knowledge into the system and teaching it how to classify information and deal with particular scenarios and decisions. This is time-consuming and labour intensive, but once the system works, it is infinitely scalable.

Robots in law – A few examples!

Although the following chapters will go into detail about the various applications of AI to the legal sector, it is worth highlighting some legal AI trailblazers.

Although litigation would seem to be the obvious starting point for legal AI, take-up by law firms has started with AI-powered virtual assistants handling discrete tasks previously carried out by trainees or junior lawyers. Other examples include legal services delivery platforms and the robotic automation of work around specific specialisms and discrete tasks.

Michael Mills of Neota Logic recently produced a MindMap of AI in law, which has been updated prior to publication in this book (see Figure 1). Mills classifies legal AI into five categories – legal research, expert automation, prediction, contract analytics, and e-discovery – and includes recent examples of each category. However, not all of these categories or offerings are underpinned by AI. For example, it is arguable whether some e-discovery software is true AI because it is searching for something specific, rather than recognising patterns and exceptions. Some prediction models are based on big data analytics

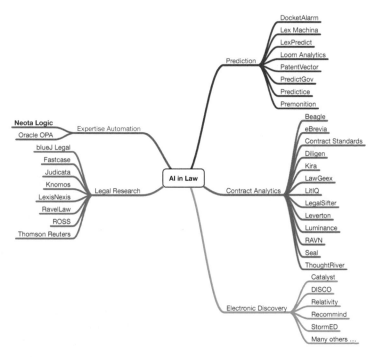

Figure 1: AI in law Mindmap. Source: Michael Mills, Neota Logic.

rather than intelligent engines – i.e. they crunch together multiple lagging variables to forecast future outcomes.

Due diligence

The hottest market for legal AI is merger and acquisition (M&A) due diligence, where there has been significant take-up by Magic Circle firms and new products are announced almost every day.

The first successful use of legal AI is LONald, the 'robotic contract lawyer' from Berwin Leighton Paisner (BLP), which supports the firm's real estate practice, handling due diligence on property transactions. It connects with the Land Registry site to verify property details and collates the results in a spreadsheet. It is powered by RAVN's Applied Cognitive Engine (ACE), a robotic platform that powers applications to organise, discover, and summarise key information from documents and unstructured data.

Kira Systems undertakes M&A due diligence by identifying and analysing clauses in company documents. It is employed by Clifford Chance to speed up deals. Kira's machine learning capability means that its competency, in terms of accuracy and speed, continuously improves as a consequence of its experience and user feedback.

Slaughter and May have teamed up with UK start-up Luminance, which is backed by Invoke Capital, run by Autonomy founder Mike Lynch, to speed up the due diligence process. It combines recursive Bayesian estimation to detect patterns in language and identify anomalies with machine learning capability. As well as analysing clauses, extracting data, and referring exceptions back to lawyers, it includes data visualisation features more commonly found in BI and big data tools.

Legal research

ROSS is a virtual knowledge worker which specialises in bankruptcy-related legal research. ROSS combines natural language processing with IBM Watson's cognitive engine and is employed by the bankruptcy practice at US law firm BakerHostetler in a professional support lawyer (PSL) role, undertaking legal research to support attorneys by finding appropriate precedents and other documents. Attorneys type in natural language questions and ROSS searches through the law and legal precedents to produce evidence-based answers.

Legal services delivery platforms

Riverview Law's Kim (knowledge, information, meaning) is an AI platform powering a range of virtual assistants that together ensure that legal work is undertaken to a consistent standard and managed efficiently. Like ROSS, Kim is built on the IBM Watson platform. It enables users to create code-free software applications for specific legal tasks and includes a triage process for allocating work appropriately.

Neota Logic is an expert system, an AI platform for creating code-free apps for applying legislation and regulation to legal queries, encapsulating legal knowledge, reasoning, and judgement to provide self-service real-time legal advice. Taylor Wessing used Neota Logic to develop an interactive app that clients can use to find out in real-time whether they are subject to the People with Significant Control (PSC) Rules. This makes legal advice infinitely scalable as it can be delivered concurrently to an unlimited number of parties.

Extending access to justice
Scalability underpins AI's potential to extend legal services to people who have been failed by the justice system. March 2016 saw London's first LegalTech Hackathon, which was organised by Legal Geek to help Hackney Community Law Centre deliver more cost-effective legal advice. The Hackathon, which was won by Fresh Innovate, a team from Magic Circle firm Freshfields Bruckhaus Deringer, produced AI-powered tools including a triage service for incoming queries and a comprehensive case management solution built on the Neota Logic platform.

Joshua Browder's DoNotPay.co.uk is a free-to-access chatbot which has challenged some £3 million in parking tickets.[6] His latest ventures provide online basic advice to help homeless people find emergency accommodation and to help tenants ensure their landlords undertake essential repairs. His next project will focus on immigration and legal advice to refugees. Browder's chatbots are extending access to the law, and highlighting accountability under specific regulations. They enable people to exercise their legal rights without prohibitive financial outlay, which in turn forces local authorities, landlords, and soon immigration authorities, to take their responsibilities seriously because more people have the ability to challenge their decisions and actions (or inactions).

The extending AI patchwork
The business model for legal AI at the moment is narrow and

specific. It follows the example of driverless cars – shuttle pods operate successfully at Heathrow Airport's Terminal 5 because they operate in a dedicated space, so all possible scenarios are covered in terms of space and content. RAVN'S Peter Wallqvist explains: 'If you define a sufficiently narrow domain in which to operate, you are more likely to be successful. At RAVN we have concentrated our robotic ability to understand documents on specific domains. Although our patchwork is big, and growing, we are not trying to create a master AI that covers everything.'

Other successful robots in law follow a similar pattern, and are limited to specific tasks. Other recent developments are narrower still, tackling particular specialisms and functions. Examples include TrademarkNow which uses AI to speed up trademark search, analysis, and protection.[7] Microsystems' 'artificial document intelligence' automatically corrects language, format, and cross-references. Like RAVN, these are about speeding up and simplifying discrete tasks.

The potential to create a 'master AI' in legal is likely to include applying cognitive engines to data analytics – an intelligent extension of BI. Law firms are increasingly driven by data, relying on BI and big data techniques to leverage management information. Chapter 2 outlines the journey from BI to AI in legal practice management.

References

1. Aibusiness.org.
2. Artificiallawyer.com.
3. McCarthy, J., Minsky, M.L., Rochester, N., and Shannon, C.E. 'A proposal for the Dartmouth summer research project on Artificial Intelligence', 31 August 1955. Available at: www-formal.stanford.edu/jmc/history/dartmouth/dartmouth.html. See also: 'Dartmouth Artificial Intelligence (AI) Conference', www.livinginternet.com/i/ii_ai.htm.
4. Bellman, R. *An Introduction to Artificial Intelligence: Can Computers Think?*, San Francisco: Boyd & Fraser Pub Co., 1978.
5. Ranger, S. 'Three reasons why AI is taking off right now (and what you need to do about it)', *ZDNet*, 27 May 2016. Available at: www.zdnet.com/article/three-reasons-why-ai-is-taking-off-right-now-and-what-you-need-to-do-about-it.
6. Donotpay.co.uk.
7. Trademarknow.com.

Chapter 2:
From BI to AI

Legal AI is more than applying mathematical forecasting techniques to real-time data. This chapter looks at the journey from business intelligence (BI) to artificial intelligence (AI) and how mainstream technology offerings related to data capture and analysis provide a jumping off point for legal AI.

It is said, 'if you can't measure it, you can't manage it', and legal practice management has for some time focused on capturing management information in real time and presenting it in a way that provides insights into the business and opportunities to improve productivity and performance. Popular legal practice management systems including LexisNexis, Thomson Reuters Elite, Aderant, and Peppermint feature business intelligence capability. Specialist BI software provided by C24, DW Reporting, and QlikView among others captures financial and performance metrics from across the business and presents them back to management and fee-earners in real time, highlighting progress against key performance indicators and guiding decision making. BI, data analysis, and content management are the foundations of legal AI.

Law firms are for-profit organisations, so leveraging management information is a key driver of BI. Financial data is presented in a way that identifies which matters, clients, and sectors are most profitable, and which lawyers are recording the highest number of billable hours and earning the most money for the firm. Client billing and other data can inform business development and client relationship management. Business intelligence supports classic management techniques including business process management, Lean

Six Sigma, and agile working, which boost productivity and efficiency by identifying and dealing with bottlenecks as well as highlighting best practices and rolling them out across the business.

An important benefit of BI is that the data can be broken down in a multitude of ways to support different roles – for example, fee-earners can look at their own billing by matter, over time, and against their targets, and can compare their performance with others, whereas a partner leading a practice area could look at billing or other indicators for their whole department and then break it down by sector, matter, client, team, or fee-earner. Business support departments such as finance, HR, or business development would focus on different metrics according to their strategic priorities.

The BI 'dashboard' is tailored to the user's profile and gives an 'at a glance' overview of the firm's key metrics. Lawyers can then drill down into the data to discover, for example, how they or their team or department are doing compared with a previous time period, their peers, or other benchmarks determined by the firm's system. BI applications can be configured to identify common business issues and potential solutions.

BI and big data

More recently law firms have been leveraging external data too. This is less about business efficiency, and more about supporting strategic decision making in a more outward-facing way than BI. Big data was the legal IT buzzword that preceded innovation and AI – and it is now part of the law firm technology architecture to the extent that some larger law firms employ business analysts and data scientists. Big data analytics apply complex algorithms to large anonymised data sets which are cut and combined in different ways to identify patterns, highlight opportunities and risks, and predict trends. In the past few years, firms have been applying big data analytics to legal work, often with the aim of minimising risk and identifying expertise.

Although the obvious differentiator is volume, big data analytics is commonly described as comprising five Vs: volume, variety, velocity, veracity, and visualisation. A sixth feature that is particularly relevant to law firms (in terms of investment decisions and partner involvement as well as market intelligence and business performance) is value. Big data analysis requires specialist tools and applications that are designed to analyse large volumes of data quickly and effectively and present the outputs in a meaningful way; therefore, as well as specific skillsets, law firm (and ABS) decision makers need to be able to demonstrate to partners and stakeholders how it will produce a return on investment (ROI) in relation to improving productivity, winning cases, expanding client services, and boosting margins. These value considerations apply equally to legal AI.

Although BI and big data analytics combine data from various sources to support strategic and operational decision making, there are important differences relating to their positioning in the business. Derek Southall, head of innovation and digital at Gowling WLG, extends the dashboard imagery by describing BI as the firm's speedometer – an essential indicator that presents internal structured data back to those who are driving the business in real time. Southall is among those who believe that law firms are only just getting to grips with BI.

Whereas BI applications analyse and present financial and management information from multiple repositories and perspectives within the business, big data analytics relate the firm's strategic direction and planning to external factors: the business environment and customer behaviour. The data, which can include internal management information as well as transactional and customer data and data from external sources, can be cut in different ways – i.e. by geography, market, sector or product, or any other combination – depending on the purpose of the exercise. Continuing Southall's analogy, where BI is the speedometer, measuring performance in real time, big data analytics is the satnav that shows you where you are in relation to your environment and the weight of traffic around you, keeps a record of recent journeys, and helps you decide on the best route to your destination!

Big data analytics have been applied successfully to volume legal services. For example, at DWF a team of analysts uses big data software to identify potentially fraudulent insurance claims. Berrymans Lace Mawer (BLM) applies big data analytics to claims data, and feeds back the findings directly to its insurance clients.

Data visualisation, which is a graphical representation of large volume data patterns, is an important part of big data analytics. Like BI's dashboards, the purpose is to make the results of the analysis easy to access and understand, which it certainly is in comparison with spreadsheets!

In 2014, Wright Hassall IT director Martyn Wells introduced C24's Bi24 business intelligence and analytics platform to support the firm's debt recovery business. A geo-demographic heat map identifies which locations have a higher propensity to pay and the recovery team concentrates its efforts on these areas, significantly improving its success rates. This drives decision making on how to proceed with particular cases – there is not much point in pursuing a case that is unlikely to produce results.

A blend of big data analytics and BI guides Wright Hassall's strategic decision making around expansion and process improvement, by applying big data techniques to industry areas in which the firm operates – and new ones it is considering moving into. The BI platform handles natural language queries (a key element of AI) to identify data clusters – for example, how many conveyancing instructions the firm is handling. Users can then drill down into the detail, splitting the data by location, property type, price, etc. While client dashboards give clients real-time access to the progress of their matters, data analytics are also applied to internal processes to identify bottlenecks, prevent the build-up of work in progress (WIP) and lock-in, and support work allocation and team management.

Big data analytics are used to identify patterns and trends in dispute resolution to predict the probability of case outcomes. In the US, LexisNexis' Lex Machina applies analytics to IP transactions and litigation, bringing together case information, court records, and other public data to predict case outcomes. Toby Unwin's Premonition analyses public data in order to identify the best lawyers to instruct for particular cases – i.e. the ones who have the most experience and the highest success rates.

BI and predictive data analysis, together with advanced search technology that handles natural language (or close to natural language) queries, are the jumping off point for legal AI because they interrogate large data sets quickly and present the results in way that supports decision making. They support AI, but they are not AI.

AI's two-factor authentication

So what is legal AI? It is worth considering what differentiates AI in the law firm context. It is generally agreed that this comes down to two main applications: machine learning (or cognitive computing) and natural language processing (NLP).

As Peter Wallqvist, CEO of RAVN Systems, explains, the main difference between BI and AI is that BI applies defined rules to structured data, while AI extracts and interprets unstructured data. As you add more data and rules, the BI system improves – and the quality of output is governed by the accuracy and validity of the data and the clarity of the rules.

'While BI derives insights from cluster analysis or regression analysis and can execute decisions against an algorithm, it cannot learn the consequences of those actions and apply that learning to future decisions', adds Wells at Wright Hassall.

AI applies machine learning to (structured or) unstructured data. Natural language processing (NLP) allows systems to respond to natural language (or close to natural language) queries – i.e. users do not have to use particular search terms and meaning is not defined purely by terminology. The system needs to be trained in the first place – in the same way a person does – and improves its output by learning from experience and feedback.

RAVN chief technology officer Jan Van Hoecke adds that while BI applies across a firm's business metrics, RAVN's AI-powered ACE is applied to narrow domains, including AI-powered search, transactional due diligence, commercial contracts, structured finance, and banking agreements; and handles discrete contextual tasks which may require recognising a variety of terminology, such as reading through contracts to discover whether they are affected by specific legislative changes. RAVN uses its own technology to identify new domains to extend its patchwork of coverage.

'BI requires data points – to identify which department has the highest billing, or how many hours particular departments or fee-earners put in to achieve a particular outcome or margin', says Van Hoecke. 'This means someone has had to identify specific data points such as the number of hours worked and the charge-out rate. BI and big data analysis break down massive data sets to identify patterns and correlations and use visualisation to make them comprehensible. But you still have to interpret the results. AI reads the data and interprets it.' He adds that NLP means that data does not have to be classified and machine learning allows the system to interpret the data by applying its training and previous interactions, and then to define a course of action.

BI and big data analytics use data that is structured in terms of meaning, whether or not it is classified – although big data sets are anonymised, some classification is required for big data analytics to produce useful results. For example, medical information will classify patients by gender, age, geography – whichever variables support the purpose of the research. In the commercial world, customer data will be classified by product or service, price, and perhaps by payment type or whether something was bought online or in store.

In the same way, big data applied to legal work is directed at particular practice areas or types of work and the results are interpreted and used to support decision making. Big data analysis does not interpret the results and define a recommended course of action, although the results may flag up a particular issue or indicate a direction that is likely to achieve the desired outcome. The next step is to add in AI – first to pull together all relevant information to guide decision making and then to create workflows to apply those decisions.

However, when you introduce AI the algorithm does more than simply apply analytics to data; once the AI engine has been trained to carry out a task, it takes decisions by mimicking what a person would do and applying the appropriate action. Van Hoecke emphasises another important quality – legal AI in particular needs to be good at identifying exceptions, the instances when the AI engine needs to pass on a decision to a lawyer. 'It is important that lawyers are confident that the system can provide answers to queries, and take decisions, but that it can also recognise the documents and queries that it cannot handle', he explains. This is another critical difference between BI and AI. RAVN's ACE marks documents that it cannot decide on in a different colour and sends them to a workflow for a lawyer to review. It creates real-time metrics estimating its own accuracy – the percentage of exceptions that it is flagging up. Wallqvist adds that this metric indicates whether it might be worth creating another robot to deal with common exceptions.

At Gowling WLG, Southall agrees that AI is differentiated by the fact that it works with unstructured data 'While BI looks at structured data and gives you the outputs that you require, AI makes sense of random information', he observes. 'While there will always be a need for structured data analysis, we're probably going to end up relying less on BI than AI because the amount of unstructured data being produced is phenomenal, exponential, and challenging.'

The AI of BI – and the BI of AI!

Eric Hunter, director of knowledge, technology, and innovation strategies at Bradford & Barthel LLP in San Diego is blending big data forecasting and predictive analytics with BI to enhance the firm's day-to-day operations. Hunter heads up the firm's spin-off consultancy, Spherical Models, which mines client and case data to predict case outcomes. This facilitates decision making – for example whether to pursue a case or to settle – and shortens the litigation process, allowing the firm to handle more work and price competitively. Visualisation creates a user-friendly interface.

Hunter is working on potentially using AI to add new dimensions to BI, for example by monitoring the tone of communication and recording user preferences in the same way YouTube does. He explains that adding this new intelligence creates what could be termed 'AI-powered BI', 'by introducing subtle intelligence that helps ensure the business is going in the right direction – and that is at the heart of BI'.

Hunter also underlines the importance of 'the BI of AI': it is critical to monitor the effectiveness of AI applications that incorporate machine learning, in terms of efficiency and their impact on the business. 'Machine learning means that we can no longer divorce process from technology', says Hunter. 'If we want to achieve something as business leaders, we have to understand precisely how and where new developments impact the business. We need to run BI on AI to make sure it is working towards our strategic and operational objectives.'

Get the BI right first

Oz Benamram, chief knowledge officer at White & Case, believes that thus far 'robots' in law are a productivity tool – narrow AI that automates routine tasks. 'It is still a rules-based engine if it follows a scripted process that involves checking information against particular websites and adding it to a list', he says. 'We need to identify the desired outcome beyond auto-mating tasks and work backwards from that. BI will transform into AI when it can connect all the dots in an organisation and help it work towards achieving desirable outcomes beyond automating tasks.'

Benamram explains that for a law firm the most significant desired outcome indication is profitability. Like Hunter, he believes that AI could transform BI by focusing on outcomes rather than tasks. 'If we can use AI to look at matters collectively and individually and learn commonalities of process and behaviour that increase profitability, we could use this to make high level decisions, like advising a client when to accept negotiation terms. It could also help us with work allocation – for example by indicating that putting a certain associate on a particular case would increase or reduce its chances of success. AI could help us develop true BI related to our overall strategic goal rather than one specific task, by showing us in real time how everything on the way to the desired outcome for each matter will help us or detract us from achieving it. At first we will decide whether or not to act on these indications and forecasts, but as the technology improves, we will use it to manage workflows and write decision trees. As long as people write the rules, it is BI not AI.'

At Riverview Law, CEO Karl Chapman's approach reflects this – Riverview's AI-powered virtual assistant Kim works predominantly with structured data, applying knowledge from all parts of the business to different types of legal work. Kim responds to natural language instructions, involves machine learning, and can be configured and reconfigured to particular matters. However, Kim also requires a consistent data and context layer. 'You have to get the BI right before you can apply AI', says Chapman, explaining that Riverview's system is built up from the data layer. This feels like a further development of legal practice management systems that are based on Microsoft Dynamics – whereby different systems and applications are built on the same underlying database, thereby ensuring data consistency across the business.

This is close to Benamram's vision of AI as a decision-making platform predicated on profitability, which would expand BI to all the information related to a matter in order to give it the best possible chance of success. This would change law firm operations by writing the decision tree in real time, while the narrow AI currently in use is changing day-to-day law firm operations and roles through intelligent automation supported by natural language processing and machine learning.

From dashboard to conversation

It has been suggested that narrow AI that incorporates machine learning and natural language processing capability is likely to change the way people interact with BI engines. The rapid results produced by narrow AI systems like RAVN which present their outputs in more direct – and user friendly – ways highlight the option of moving away from the BI dashboard, perhaps to a more conversational user interface. Author and commentator Nir Eyal recently suggested that intelligent software would see the end of the BI dashboard, replacing what he describes as 'an intimidating explosion of charts and graphs' with 'a conversational interface' that 'listens and learns'. Although it is unlikely that legal services will abandon the charts and graphs that help them understand the firm's key financial and operational indicators, there is a move towards a conversational interface in the form of the digital virtual assistant.

RAVN's ACE, which undertakes due diligence work, and Riverview's Kim which is an intelligent knowledge management tool, are among market entrants that apply AI-powered solutions to specific challenges related to managing the volume and content of legal documents. They combine intelligent search with big data analytics, extracting information from the content of large volumes of documents, and there is also an element of BI as context is added to information. Chapter 3 looks at the first robots in law – the digital legal assistant.

Part 2:
Putting AI to work

Chapter 3:
Legal research –
Virtual assistants

The first robots in law were virtual assistants that support due diligence and legal research. These are narrow, or applied, AI that work with particular legal specialisms, processes, and challenges. This chapter presents examples of AI-powered virtual assistants including RAVN, which was first deployed at Berwin Leighton Paisner, ROSS at BakerHostetler, and Kira Systems at Clifford Chance. These are just a few examples of an exponentially growing range of products and services in this space.

In her keynote address on 19 September 2016 to the International Bar Association conference in Washington DC, Catherine Dixon, the chief executive of the Law Society of England and Wales, said that 'technology can play a facilitative role in helping law firms achieve productivity-driven growth by increasing accuracy, saving time, and driving efficiencies'. The AI-powered virtual assistants featured in this chapter do exactly that.

As leading legal IT commentator Robert Ambrogi observed, it is interesting that although the closest legal technology to AI is e-discovery software, which can search large volumes of data for items that are relevant to a dispute, the first legal AI to hit the mainstream was on the transactional side, handling transactional due diligence rather than litigation support. One reason for this is that M&A work often involves working to very tight deadlines, with lawyers working through the night to seal a deal. Although litigation also has timetables, these tend to be set at the outset of the case; they can be amended, but this needs to be negotiated with the judge and the parties, whereas an M&A deal deal can fold or change and parties can leave and enter the fray at short notice. There is also the question of costs; transactional clients are more likely to consider the cost of due diligence as a strategic element of the deal that can be handled by a choice of different suppliers/advisors, so law firms need to demonstrate a clear business case.

Unusually for transformational legal technology, the take-up of legal AI in due diligence and contract review work tends to be led by M&A lawyers rather than by the IT function, although the latter is involved in the implementation and roll-out. Rather than having to be 'sold' the benefits of applying technology, parties to a deal are actively looking for an advantage in terms of speed, accuracy, and cost-effectiveness.

Of course, these factors are driving the expansion of due diligence/contract review from transactional to litigation work, as vendors, law firms, and corporate legal departments recognise the potential to transform e-discovery's already crowded and competitive marketplace.

Contract robots – Beyond automation

Legal AI first hit the mainstream news in 2015 when Berwin Leighton Paisner (BLP) was the first law firm to go public about its 'contract robot', which it developed in partnership with RAVN Systems. This intelligent virtual assistant was fondly named LONald by BLP's real estate team, due to its role in serving light obstruction notices. LONald conducts due diligence for real estate deals by verifying property details against the official public records.

The BBC has described BLP's LONald as a robot that could potentially replace lawyers. However, this is somewhat misleading – LONald and other legal virtual digital assistants are designed to facilitate and augment lawyers rather than supplant them, by automating and speeding up support work.

Nor is LONald a physical robot, despite its anthropomorphisation by BLP's real estate litigation group! It is a software application that automates an aspect of legal work that was previously handled by junior associates or paralegals. Powered by RAVN's ACE it automatically reads documents and unstructured data and extracts and summarises key information.

LONald supports BLP's real estate team by connecting with the Land Registry site and verifying the property details for large portfolio transactions. It extracts the relevant data and enters it into an Excel spreadsheet. It then cross-checks data points to remove duplicates and uses the data to send out queries. For example, it can send a query to Companies House, to check a company's address against financial and other information. Any discrepancies are flagged up for review by the (human) legal team.

As Matthew Whalley – BLP's former head of legal risk consultancy who spearheaded the implementation – said, once the programme has been trained to identify and work with specific variables, it can complete two weeks' work in around two seconds, making LONald over 12 million times quicker than an associate doing the same task manually! This contributes considerable savings of resource and fee-earning time to any large project. Obviously, the bigger the project the greater the benefit in terms of cost-saving and value for money.

Jan Van Hoecke, technical director at RAVN, explains that LONald runs in the cloud, so lawyers interact directly with it – giving it documents to check – without involving BLP's IT department. Although the system needs to be trained to carry out the data checks – to read and recognise the information it needs – the user interface is straightforward, requiring minimal training and no tech skills.

Wendy Miller, co-head of real estate disputes at BLP, explains how LONald supports her practice group. 'We have developed an adaptable tool which combines initial due diligence with the outputs that we require. It takes us from raw documents to a standardised, verified summary that we can manipulate and analyse.'

Rather than lawyers worrying about being 'replaced' by robots, Wendy has seen an improvement in morale within the real estate group, in particular because LONald alleviates pressure on the team by reducing fluctuations in workload. 'In a big deal, there might be hundreds of documents to analyse one week and very few the next. Previously, this meant managing staffing levels and ensuring that we paid people overtime or hired temporary staff only when we needed to – as clients do not perceive the value in data extraction, it is hard to charge out for it – whereas now we simply feed the documents into the data extraction portal and get a consistent output in terms of style and quality. And the robot doesn't get tired or bored!'

LONald, and ACE generally, goes several steps beyond sophisticated, contextual search technology. Once it has extracted the required information, it categorises its findings and presents them in a standardised and consistent way, flagging up any mismatches or potential issues. Whereas sophisticated search produces results and ranks them, but you then have to extract the information you need from the output, the RAVN system sifts for and only extracts relevant information.

RAVN CEO Peter Wallqvist explains. 'For example, a real estate lawyer might need to look through a property portfolio to find leases that were negotiated before a particular date. A search engine would find all the leases and then divide them into those that started before and after that date. The RAVN system would read the leases to find the start dates and only extract the relevant ones.' The system can do this kind of work almost instantly and perfectly accurately, whereas a person could well miss something. Scenarios which deal with closed questions like this require almost no human input, whereas others where the information might be less clearly defined are likely to find more exceptions – results that require a human decision.

Exception handling is a critical success factor, adds Van Hoecke. 'The system has to be able to recognise the documents that need to be passed on to a lawyer. It is important that lawyers are confident that the system can answer some queries, but can also recognise the documents that it cannot determine. We had that baked-in from the start.'

When the system identifies a piece of data it cannot decide on, it marks it up for review. It also estimates in real time how well it is doing with the work – i.e. what proportion of documents it is recognising and dealing with, and the proportion passed on for review. This enables the process to be redesigned and improved for maximum efficiency. 'If the exception pile becomes big enough, it is relatively straightforward to create another robot to deal with new categories', says Wallqvist.

Although BLP's LONald only handles real estate work, there are plans to roll out the process across other practice areas. RAVN's ACE can be applied to diligence work in relation to commercial contracts, structured finance, and banking agreements, including International Swaps and Derivatives Association (ISDA) master agreements, which may need to be renegotiated in line with legislative changes. 'Our AI robots can quickly check through all a firm's contracts highlighting anything that relates to a particular legislative change', says Wallqvist. A recent development was RAVN's LPP Robot which reviews documents for legal professional privilege, which may be an indication that the AI vendor is contemplating moving into the e-discovery market.

LONald converts unstructured data into structured data – i.e. a spreadsheet – that supports lawyers' work. As Wallqvist explains, the system is successful because it operates in specific narrow domains. Since the launch of LONald at BLP, more law firms have announced partnerships with RAVN, including Linklaters, Reed Smith, Travers Smith, and Danish firm Bech-Bruun. Dentons and its research and development arm, start-up accelerator NextLaw Labs, have collaborated with RAVN to produce an algorithm to identify provisions that could be impacted by Brexit (demonstrating that contract review is not just for due diligence). Documents are reviewed in order to highlight 'touchpoints' that may require further attention – including legal advice.

Linklaters and other Magic Circle firms are clearly putting their money on virtual assistants for competitive advantage through transactional due diligence and regulatory compliance. Linklaters, the first Magic Circle firm to go public with the use of AI, is working with a selection of AI companies including RAVN. Again, the focus is on due diligence, notably in relation to banking and securities work. For example, it has developed Verifi, a computer programme that can sift through 14 European and UK regulatory registers to check client names for banks. Linklaters also works with German AI vendor Leverton, which applies deep learning (a branch of machine learning that trains algorithms to recognise patterns in digital representations of sounds, images, and other data) to extract provisions from legal documents in the form of attributes rather than text. Leverton's ability to interface with enterprise resource planning (ERP) systems such as SAP, which Linklaters also uses, mean that these attributes – i.e. what a clause means rather than what it states – are language agnostic and can be accessed in 21 different languages without the need for translation. Leverton's ability to create summaries dispenses with the need to create abstracts of precedent documents, new legislation or regulations, or other relevant documentation.

At Thomson Reuters legal debate in June 2016, Linklaters partner Edward Chan spoke against the motion that AI will fail to have a radical impact on the legal profession, arguing that 'even if we focus on the machine doing only 20–30 per cent of routine legal work, AI will make a radical change in the practice of law'. Although he conceded that legal AI was currently only scratching the surface of legal work, by advancing automated workflow technology to include due diligence and legal research, its significant impact will relate to client expectations and the pricing of legal services – because law firms bill by the time taken to complete a task. 'Today's data room is virtual and has thousands of documents. AI is the only way a firm can manage that amount of data. It's not just about the 20 per cent of work you can automate – it's about managing the data to preserve the judgement.' Chan believes that AI will also reshape law firm structure, by handling routine work that is traditionally done by junior lawyers and professional support lawyers – and so will change their roles by enabling them to focus on perhaps more complex, value-added work. It may also mean firms take on fewer trainees or train them in a different way.

Chan was prompted to think about AI by the competitive pressure on fees and the need to find more efficient ways of working. He jokingly says it was FOMO – fear of missing out – on what other firms were doing that first encouraged him to take an interest. However, this is relevant in a highly competitive environment, such as panel processes, where clients are interested in two elements around technology: what technology is being used by a firm, and how much difference it makes in terms of efficiency and cost. For firms such as Linklaters, legal AI is a way of meeting the challenge of market pressure to drive efficiency and taking the opportunity to differentiate and productise its technology offering.

Kira Systems brings similar benefits to M&A due diligence. Kira belongs to another strand of trailblazing legal virtual assistants that support the work of individual lawyers in real time. Kira Systems, which handles M&A due diligence, and ROSS Intelligence, which carries out legal research, both originate from Canada – which is increasingly recognised as a legal tech start-up hot spot. Both rely heavily on machine learning – and, therefore, machine teaching.

Machine learning… and teaching

Kira Systems was developed in Toronto by former lawyer Noah Waisberg with the purpose of reducing the time and effort involved in M&A due diligence. Kira moves the virtual assistant towards becoming an expert system. Like RAVN, it uses natural language processing and machine learning. However, Kira applies specific practice-area expertise as it extracts relevant clauses from contracts for evaluation and comparison.

As Waisberg explains, due diligence in terms of M&A deals and banking and financial agreements involves looking for particular types of clause that may affect a deal, or even prevent a deal from going through. 'While due diligence is not all contract review, it is often primarily contract review, and contract review typically represents 30–60 per cent of the legal fees for handling a deal. While M&A lawyers look at the contracts and commitments of the target company, securities and capital markets lawyers look at model precedents.'

The other key component of contract review in relation to deal-making is that it has to be done accurately in a pressurised, time-poor scenario. However, although the work is repetitive and to some extent routine, it is less straightforward than verifying facts, as it also involves looking for clauses that may affect the nature of a relationship. Hence it took Kira Systems some years to develop an effective system. However, now it conducts contract review in 20–90 per cent of the time that it takes a team of junior associates and paralegals to do the same work manually, depending on the nature of the contract.

Why did Kira Systems take so long to develop? Waisberg explains that this is because its key technology is machine learning – and machine learning requires machine teaching. Because the software actually reads contracts, rather than looking for particular words and phrases, it needs to understand the content it works with. This means it needs to learn from examples – and the more contracts it reads, and the more corrections and feedback it receives from the experienced lawyers who train it, the more effective it becomes.

What do we mean by 'effectiveness' in relation to AI? Waisberg measures effectiveness by way of two metrics: accuracy and data efficiency. How accurate are the findings, and how much data do they need to achieve a useful (valuable) level of accuracy? Waisberg agrees with RAVN's Wallqvist and Van Hoecke that it is equally important, for the sake of establishing both business value and user confidence in the system, for the system to quickly and comprehensively identify and mark up instances that need to be referred back for human review. Machine learning – and machine teaching – means that as the system works with more examples and learns from user feedback, it builds an increasingly accurate and cost-effective model. Just like a human lawyer (or any expert) the system learns from being taught, applying its learning to real cases, and subsequent user feedback. Unlike a human lawyer (but in common with other robots in law), Kira is scalable. It can handle multiple cases simultaneously and learn from feedback from multiple users.

A simple benefit is that Kira saves lawyers time, so clients benefit from reduced turnaround time. It also means that lawyers can put in more billable hours and give clients better value. AI adds another valuable dimension. Because it is intelligent, the software may uncover clauses that do not fit into the initial classification, but contain information that it has deduced from its training may be relevant to the deal – i.e. the machine can pick up something that a lawyer may have missed. This can then be added to the model to create a revised model that is applied to new documents. By constantly building new models, Kira's AI software can produce results that are more accurate than human reviewers.

Kira is designed to differentiate because law firms and others adapt the system to their specific requirements. The system is pre-trained to recognise more than 100 data points – for example, you can apply it to any set of contracts and ask it to find the notice section, the terms of the agreement, or the renewal – however, like RAVN, Kira can also be customised to different practice areas and specific projects. It can be adapted according to the data that it handles, the criteria programmed into it, and importantly who is training it – i.e. adding their expertise to the mix. For example, although Kira was created for M&A lawyers, Deloitte is using it for consultancy and audit and has added over 1,000 new data points to adapt it to this purpose. Like the best knowledge systems, Kira institutionalises competitive advantage by making knowledge, know-how, and expertise scalable. This is particularly valuable to law firms, as it enables junior lawyers to benefit from the expertise of senior lawyers who help to train the system. A particular benefit for the Magic Circle and BigLaw firms that use it – which include Clifford Chance and Freshfields Bruckhaus Deringer – is that it institutionalises a firm's knowledge by capturing expertise in a practical way. Because it becomes part of Kira's training, it is automatically applied to all relevant matters. Another important benefit to any firm is when experienced practitioners leave the firm, their expertise continues to contribute to the quality of its due diligence activities and the continuing professional development of new partners and associates.

Bas Boris Visser, global head of innovation and business change at Clifford Chance, first encountered Kira on a fact-finding trip to New York, where he was looking into e-discovery technology. Visser sees parallels between the use of technology assisted review (TAR) in litigation and applying AI technology to transactional due diligence. Whereas eight or ten years ago most lawyers were sceptical about TAR, now it is the de facto approach – judges demand it and client companies tend to have their preferred technology providers.

Visser emphasises that developments in the transactional space are also driven by client demand – due to time and cost pressures. It is also about Clifford Chance using technology to maintain its market-leading position as a Magic Circle transactional firm, and hopefully gaining some competitive advantage.

Visser's comments echo Chan at Linklaters. 'It is key for us to be right on top of the latest developments', he says. 'I don't want to wake up one day to find out that part of the work we used to do is now done by a computer that is not on our desks and we are not doing it too because we thought it would not work!'

This view is reflected by many in the broader AI community and was repeated by numerous commentators at the AI Summit in San Francisco in September 2016. Unlike other game changers, such as mobile, where fast followers have benefited from the lessons learned by early adopters, AI is one of those technologies where it pays to be a first mover – because machine learning means that the system is continually improving as it learns from every matter and transaction. This means that early adopters' systems will be better trained than those of their competitors. 'For clients, the fact that we are training it and working with it is highly appreciated at a time when they are under huge pressure to reduce legal spend', says Visser.

Another advantage of introducing AI into routine processes is the potential to broaden the business, enabling Magic Circle firms to take on volume work from clients who instruct them on business-critical deals because RAVN, Kira Systems, and others offer them a way to do volume work cost-effectively without compromising on quality.

Visser sees the customisable element of Kira Systems as offering the potential of scalable competitive advantage. 'It arrives with some data and training, but our lawyers need to test whether it recognises the things they need to recognise and in the right way. The next step is to train it ourselves so that it includes clauses and provisions that are specific to Clifford Chance and our clients.'

In this way, AI can be used to reflect and enhance the brand. 'Anybody can buy Kira, but not everyone can buy Kira as programmed by Clifford Chance', says Visser. 'The challenge is to find lawyers to train it, invest in it, and make it our product – and work with clients who are interested in seeing what it can do for them. Most clients are happy to help us make it work.'

'Whereas e-discovery tools can understand what a document is about and work out whether it is potentially relevant to an investigation, tools like Kira go deeper inside the document, so that data can be extracted for different purposes. You can use it for due diligence, for example, by instructing it to find the change of control clause in different documents and putting them into a report. Every time it finds the right clause it gets better at recognising them. It is therefore constantly maintaining and expanding its – and the firm's – knowledge, enabling us to extend the basic system into a Clifford Chance proprietary product.'

The Clifford Chance brand helps engage clients with the AI tools. 'It's quicker and easier for clients to become comfortable with these products when they are validated by Clifford Chance and carry the Clifford Chance brand than they would with a small start-up for example, even if it offered comparable products and services. Our quality and expertise are our key selling points and underpin our reputation, so we need to make the product our own and make sure it reflects our brand. Our automated due diligence products need to be able to do what our lawyers can do, and differentiate our brand in the same way as they do, so they require a lot of input from our lawyers. We need to give it our signature and ensure it reflects our unique capabilities and expertise.'

Clifford Chance is rolling out Kira in multiple departments – M&A is a no brainer, and it is also relevant to the real estate and funds practices – and machine learning can help the departments to learn from each other and benefit from each other's learning. Visser is also looking at combining Kira's AI-powered contract review with big data analysis to support M&A decision making. 'People talk a lot about costs, which are important from an investment decision, but it is also about enhancing the quality and added value of a due diligence exercise. For example, parties to M&A deals often talk about the synergies between companies, but often by combining the target company's data with the purchasing company's data, these are not always true synergies.'

Contract review is sometimes done by sampling – looking at a limited number of contracts and extrapolating the results – because looking at them all is too expensive and time consuming. But this technology can improve predictive valuation and risk assessment – instead of looking at 10 per cent of the data and assessing the risk, you could look at the whole data set and calculate the risk. 'From a qualitative perspective, the technology will move the needle', observes Visser. 'It's about cost saving, but the qualitative upside is where we and our clients see the value.'

Visser highlights the value of AI in the compliance space. 'We automate complex processes in the regulatory space, where clients need to show they are complying with multiple rules and regulations. Compliance is becoming extremely difficult from a value perspective.'

Machine learning – and machine teaching – requires a long-term commitment to investing time and money in the system. Moreover, according to Visser, 'investing in this type of technology is very much a consensus decision because it involves a lot of people – within the firm and also our clients – to make it work'.

Client wins for Kira Systems in 2016 include Silicon Valley law firm Fenwick & West, Osler in Canada, and Irish firm McCann FitzGerald.

The conversational assistant

ROSS Intelligence takes the virtual assistant role further, into specialist legal research, by blending machine learning with natural language processing (NLP). ROSS has been described as 'the world's first robot lawyer'. It is a genuine virtual assistant – like Siri you can ask it natural language questions and it searches for answers. Like RAVN, Kira, and others, it is trained so that it has specific legal expertise. As of 2016, ROSS is a bankruptcy lawyer – but it is being trained to cover other practice areas.

ROSS (owned by ROSS Intelligence) combines IBM Watson's cognitive computing with the natural language capabilities of Apple's Siri. As CEO and co-founder Andrew Arruda explains: 'We combine third-party AI technology with our own applications – we buy what's out there and build onto it to give it the capability we need.'

ROSS, which is accessed as an online subscription service, was developed in Canada and trained on Canadian labour and employment laws. Having secured backing as the first investment for Dentons NextLaw Labs, it moved to Silicon Valley and its first product was based on US bankruptcy law. ROSS hit the headlines early in 2016 when its virtual assistant was employed by national US firm BakerHostetler in its bankruptcy practice.

It is used by Dentons, and subsequent client wins include international firm Latham and Watkins, US national firm Womble Carlyle, and regional firm von Brieson.

ROSS carries out a professional support lawyer (PSL) role, undertaking legal research. It supports attorneys by finding appropriate precedents and other documents and answering legal questions that relate to the matters they handle. As Arruda explains, rather than typing in a word or phrase, you can ask ROSS a natural language question – in the same way as a junior lawyer might consult a more experienced colleague/partner. For example, you could ask: 'What is the difference between set off and recruitment?' ROSS then reads through the law and legal precedents, gathers evidence, draws inferences, and returns an evidence-based answer.

Although ROSS can be programmed to include voice recognition and voice-to-text capability, lawyers usually prefer to type their queries rather than speaking to the computer. But this is likely to change as virtual assistants like Apple's Siri, Microsoft's Cortana, Amazon's Alexa, and Google's Assistant become more widely used in business, and Arruda is building a mobile version of ROSS with a voice interface. As well as being useful for remote and mobile working, this could well be useful for meetings, where ROSS could be asked to find and read out excerpts from a relevant precedent or other documents. The voice interface is likely to appeal to millennials and Arruda has established a partnership with Vanderbilt Law School to give ROSS to students. He is also working on potentially adding avatars to give ROSS a more human, user-friendly interface.

ROSS incorporates supervised and unsupervised machine learning. 'Our legal specialists have trained ROSS and helped to point it towards appropriate answers to various questions', explains Arruda. 'The feedback loop is key. We encourage users to up-vote and down-vote passages to confirm or deny ROSS's interpretation of the question. Every time a user interacts with ROSS and adds feedback, the system becomes smarter – and more bespoke to the organisation.'

Like RAVN and Kira, ROSS requires training to operate in each practice area – because it needs specific knowledge – and to be aligned with the way the firm operates. Once that significant investment in time and resource has been made, the system continues to improve itself, becoming more knowledgeable and more accurate – better at finding the right information first time. Like Kira, as well as supporting individual lawyers in their day-to-day work, ROSS helps institutionalise the firm's knowledge, so that when a rainmaker moves firms or a senior partner retires, their knowledge and expertise is ingrained in the system. Arruda explains that, like Facebook, ROSS extends its knowledge as more lawyers use the system – and as it interfaces with internal and external knowledge repositories.

Although ROSS has been described as having the potential to 'replace' lawyers, like the other virtual assistants described in this chapter, it is designed rather to augment their work. 'When you have AI working alongside a human it speeds up the human's ability to learn too as the AI teaches the human who is training it. Sometimes people think of it as a static tool, but having access to a system that doesn't sleep and eat and is always there to help improves the human's output and performance too', says Arruda. This highlights its potential to support smaller firms, particularly specialist boutiques and solo practitioners, who may not necessarily be able or willing to take on more staff. ROSS enables them to take on more work by giving them a scalable PSL. For bigger firms it enhances productivity and competitive advantage because, like Kira, the system learns from the experience of the whole firm and all its lawyers, so each firm that uses ROSS is creating a different, bespoke system that is tailored to its practice and its clients.

BakerHostetler is now applying ROSS beyond its bankruptcy practice to other practice areas, including intellectual property and employment. Arruda explains that this will allow the system to work firm-wide and apply its expertise across multiple practice areas, enabling them to learn automatically from each other's experience. This is a first step to legal AI becoming broader (although it is still fulfilling a particular role – supporting legal research). ROSS is covering more practice areas and sharing knowledge and learning across those practice areas. 'We used bankruptcy law as a test area and ROSS learned how to be a good researcher in common law, so as we add different specialisms, ROSS can carry that learning from one practice area to another', adds Arruda.

Machine learning is at the heart of legal AI

Machine learning – and machine teaching – is time consuming, and it is a continual process. However, once the system is up and running – and learning – it offers early-adopter firms immediate and potential significant competitive advantage that is tailored to their particular practices and expertise. It brings significant time savings without any compromise on accuracy or quality and makes a firm's knowledge scalable.

On the other hand, because AI leverages data, data assets become the key to competitive advantage. This presents interesting possibilities and challenges to the big legal publishers who hold vast quantities of data. The fact that the biggest technology companies and publishers are buying and investing in data-rich organisations demonstrates that they recognise data as a currency for competitive advantage and are working to enhance and leverage their existing data. So legal AI must also involve data as an asset that needs to be nurtured and maintained in order to produce a compound return on investment.

Machine learning is at the heart of all these systems, and it represents both a challenge and an opportunity. A key challenge, as mentioned, is that machine learning also entails machine teaching, and training a bespoke system that covers a lot of detail and incorporates in-depth expertise requires time and resources, as Professor Katie Atkinson explained in Chapter 1. For law firms that measure value in terms of time, whether they charge out by the hour or work for fixed and capped fees, time is literally money. So a case has to be made (internally, and potentially involving clients too, depending on the seniority of the lawyer and whether they are handling ongoing work for particular clients) for taking lawyers off fee-earning work in order to train the system. There is also the question of integration with a firm's structure in terms of roles and responsibilities as well as IT architecture. For example, although RAVN is cloud-based so it does not involve BLP's IT department in terms of installation and support, it still needs to be integrated with the firm's processes and working practices so that people know it is available and how to use it, and strategically so that it can be applied wherever it can benefit the firm.

The solution is for legal AI to follow the example of other sectors that recognise that machine teaching doesn't necessarily have to happen on-site. One of the key opportunities of AI and machine learning is scalability – due diligence engines read multiple documents simultaneously and the entire system learns from everything they read. When a driverless car is involved in an incident or accident, the software is configured in such a way that the entire fleet learns from each individual incident, there is potential for law firms and clients to combine knowledge resources in a broader way, although this could raise ethical, confidentiality, and compliance issues.

Although virtual assistants that support specific legal practices are not entirely off-the-shelf products, due diligence AI is gearing up to hit the mainstream – with the launch of self-service AI products from RAVN and Luminance. The following chapter heralds the emergence of AI-powered 'driverless law'.

Chapter 4:
'Driverless' law – An intelligent platform for legal services

This chapter looks at the development of 'AI as a service' in legal, including the first robot lawyers! These reflect the development of AI platforms and conversational commerce in other industry sectors. We consider the concept of 'driverless' law in terms of white-labelled intelligent contract creation, as well as the introduction of on-demand AI-powered services that support legal services delivery, such as data extraction for due diligence and to support cross-jurisdictional transactions.

The combination of the commoditisation of legal services and a liberalised legal services marketplace has produced self-service law like Rocket Lawyer and Legal Zoom. These customer-facing applications are based on automated workflows, like a wizard, where you enter details into forms to produce a tailored version of a standard legal document, such as a basic contract or a will. Rocket Lawyer allows you to ask legal questions which are answered by experts and, if you need further help, there is a database of local lawyers offering discounted legal fees through the Rocket Lawyer site. Legal Zoom offers similar services in the US and is about to launch in the UK. AI-powered conversational commerce in the form of virtual assistants and chatbots has taken this forward with the rise of 'robot lawyers' and stand-alone subscription platforms that have produced AI as a service (AIaaS) for legal services providers and their customers.

Robot lawyers – The legal chatbot

AI – and the rise of conversational commerce – has led to a new breed of automated customer-facing legal services – the robot lawyer! These are online chatbots – a chatbot, or conversational agent, is a programme which carries out a simulated conversation with human website users, generating replies to live queries.

The first one to hit the UK market was DoNotPay, a free chatbot created by 20-year-old entrepreneur and Stanford University student Joshua Browder to appeal parking tickets. Since it was launched in August 2015, Browder's DoNotPay chatbot has successfully challenged some 200,000 parking fines by applying rules and regulations to live queries. Basically, it allows motorists to select a valid defence and enter the relevant details. It then automatically generates a customised appeal, which it sends to the council responsible for issuing the ticket.

Browder's next step was to expand his fleet of 'robot lawyers' from parking fines to homelessness. 'Following the success of the robot in appealing parking tickets, I received a large number of messages about evictions and repossessions, which are at the highest levels ever recorded', he said.

The result is a chatbot that helps homeless people claim public housing. It is based on an algorithm which applies attributes and trends in successful application letters to live cases. 'It works by asking questions to ensure the person is eligible before requesting specific details, which it uses to generate a legally sound housing application that can be sent directly to the local authorities', he said.

Browder is also expanding the service to help Syrian asylum seekers to apply for refugee status in the UK, with a bot that answers questions in Arabic but produces documents in English.

Browder's next project will 'democratise' the ability to create bots, by developing a tool that will enable law firms to build their own chatbots. 'I believe that a large number of legal documents can be automated', he said, 'so I am building a tool that requires no technical knowledge to create a bot in exchange for a link back to the firm's website. This will enable me to expand the service from half a dozen bots to a thousand.' In effect this will create the UK's first automated law firm.

Like RAVN and the virtual assistants featured in the previous chapter, each of Browder's bots requires development time, which includes consultation and collaboration with lawyers. 'It's quite a long process. They identify an issue and I then decide whether it is technically possible to automate the process. The next step is to prepare the legal documents. I want to take away the friction and automate the process.'

Browder has received approaches from several US law firms and predicts a similar level of interest from UK legal services providers. He is also working with several legal-focused charities in the UK, including two housing and homelessness charities, Shelter and Centrepoint, to create bots.

Although Browder's chatbots provide legal advice, are they replacing lawyers? Probably not, because most people would not use a lawyer to challenge a parking ticket – the legal advice might be more expensive than the ticket. The same applies to some landlord repairs.

However, Browder's bots are extending access to the law, and highlighting obligations and accountability. His website makes it worthwhile and cost-effective to challenge parking tickets and make landlords carry out necessary repairs to their properties. This is practical altruism because it enables people to exercise their legal rights without prohibitive financial outlay. Hopefully, this will encourage local authorities and landlords – and soon immigration authorities – to take their responsibilities seriously by making it easier for people to challenge unfair or incorrect penalties, decisions, and actions (or inactions).

Browder is strongly aware of the ethical and potential liability issues around chatbots taking or guiding decisions and he is building into the DoNotPay system an approval process whereby lawyers check the chatbot's responses on an ongoing basis, to ensure they always remain valid and appropriate.

LawBot, which was launched in November 2016, applies a similar principle to criminal law. The brainchild of four law students at the University of Cambridge, LawBot is a chatbot that provides free advice to victims of crime. LawBot covers 26 criminal offences and has a slightly different focus. It is not designed to replace advice from a lawyer or to take the case forward;

the idea is to help people find out how the law applies to their situation – for example, whether they have been the victim of a crime – and to provide a preliminary assessment and guidance on what to do next, from locating the nearest police station to seeking professional legal advice. The first offence LawBot tackled was sexual assault, where victims may find it easier in the first instance to consult a machine rather than make an official statement, particularly if sensitive issues such as consent are involved. 'LawBot is as empathetic as humanly possible', says a press release, adding that the questions and responses were written in consultation with therapists and psychologists.

These examples both highlight the need for the continued involvement of lawyers and other experts – in terms of assessment and approvals – in legal chatbots, as in all conversational commerce. The next step may be a chatbot that recognises when to refer a case on to a human advisor.

From document automation to driverless law

Law firms have been using document automation tools to create templates and workflows for several years. These can be white labelled to create customer-facing self-service resources – i.e. customers fill in a form to create a standard document, or to open a new matter, so that the lawyer they instruct has the information required to progress the case. Corporate lawyers can productise this service too. Berwin Leighton Paisner (BLP) uses Thomson Reuters' ContractExpress to offer its commercial construction clients the ability to produce their own documents, or suites of documents, automatically while benefiting from BLP's expertise and technology investments. ContractExpress manages the entire contract process, including approval layers (and non-standard terms) and third-party applications such as e-signature capability. Because some of the processing is outside the system, there is potential to extend the workflow to include AI-powered tools to customise contract creation.

AI as a service (AIaaS) takes this concept further, applying AI in a narrower, more specialised way to contract creation, using benchmarking and the firm's knowledge resources and specific expertise – for example, by incorporating standard clauses and clauses used in similar contracts.

This development could be described as 'driverless' law because it is analogous to the evolutionary way that 'driverless' or 'autonomous' vehicles are appearing on public roads. We are not moving suddenly from a scenario where most, if not all, vehicles travelling on public highways have someone driving – and if there is just one person in a vehicle, they are the driver – to a futuristic scenario where cars with no driver at all are autonomously taking passengers from one place to another. In the same way, we are unlikely to see an overnight transformation in the way legal work is carried out so that human intervention becomes unnecessary.

To take the car analogy further, cars today record a lot of data, which can be used, for example, to reduce insurance premiums for careful drivers, or to ascertain whether the cause of an accident was due to a technical failure or driver error. In the same way, automated workflows and applications produce data that can be analysed and used to improve – or further automate – processes by re-using knowledge, information, and know-how. For example, ContractExpress offers the ability to review transactional information within documents, and a predictive as-you-type tool suggests what to include when creating rules.

Self-driving platforms?

Another element of 'driverless' law is the development of self-service systems. Whereas the first 'robots' to handle legal work were developed with law firms to meet specific needs, the next iteration – self-service applications – are making legal AI significantly more accessible and affordable.

As these are external resources, they do not need to integrate with firms' existing systems, and, in common with other cloud applications, they can be deployed only when they are required. These systems combine standardised applications with user configuration and control.

One such service is RAVN's self-service portal, Extract Direct, which is a pay-as-you-go version of Extract, RAVN's due diligence software for contract analysis and document review. BLP's LONald (featured in the previous chapter) was an early example, and RAVN has since developed a variety of bespoke AI-powered applications based on its Applied Cognitive Engine (ACE) for numerous firms. However, these are relatively time-consuming projects as RAVN needs to work closely with each firm to develop and train the system so that it is tailored to meet their specific requirements and ways of working.

Extract Direct gives firms more control over training the robot and configuring it to their requirements – i.e. the type of documents it needs to read, and what needs to be extracted. Obviously, this will vary according to the nature of the matter and the way the tool is being used – for example, whether data extraction and document comparison is used to renew contracts or leases, to conduct M&A due diligence, or to facilitate compliance. However, this assumes some competence within the firm in terms of working with AI – or at least with contract automation technology. BLP is among the firms that employ a dedicated document automation manager. Some firms, however, are looking for an AI-powered tool that they can use when it is needed, without having to train the system first – hence the rise of 'pay-as-you-go AI'.

Pay-as-you-go AI

Luminance, backed by Innovate Capital (owned by Autonomy founder Mike Lynch) delivers exactly that. (RAVN's founders are also Autonomy alumni.)

Luminance is a document analysis tool that is used for due diligence. CEO Emily Foges explains that Luminance is different from other due diligence tools because it is not an attempt to improve existing processes and make them more efficient. Rather it works directly from the raw data, reading large volumes of documents simultaneously and identifying similarities and anomalies.

Unlike bespoke virtual assistants (e.g. RAVN, Kira Systems, ROSS), which need to be trained by the supplier and subsequently by the law firm, the machine learning element is done in-house by Luminance, not by the firms who use its online services. Its website promises an immediate and global overview of any company, picking out warning signs without needing any instruction.

How is this possible? Foges explains that Luminance combines supervised and unsupervised learning. The unsupervised learning is the machine reading and comparing documents and categorising them according to their identical and similar qualities. The supervised learning is the classification – i.e. identifying whether a certain type of document is a sales agreement or an employment contract. It can then drill down and look at clauses within the documents in a contextual way, using natural language processing, which would enable it, for example, to select all clauses that cover compliance even if they don't contain compliance-related vocabulary.

Like RAVN, the strength of Luminance lies in its ability to spot anomalies – i.e. to identify which agreements are different from others in the same category. Because it highlights anomalies immediately, it identifies risk very early in the process. 'This could kill a deal', explains Foges, 'but because it would be at an earlier stage than if traditional due diligence were applied, it would save the parties expenses on taking the deal forward only to have it fall through later when due diligence uncovered something that proved to be a deal breaker.' Luminance immediately identifies which documents are different and what makes them different – i.e. whether they are a 'smoking gun' or a 'deal breaker'.

Luminance combines a different approach to data analytics with big data visualisation. Using computer vision capability, Luminance can read and interpret photos and diagrams from PowerPoint slides or photographs of old documents as well as electronic data, and it can highlight anomalies like documents with pages missing. So, the anomalies it identifies are not just within the data; they could be about the data.

Luminance is not configured for individual firms. 'Unlike e-discovery engines, Luminance has no preconceptions about what it's looking for', adds Foges. 'You don't need to give it instructions at the outset because it surfaces what's in the data room. Visualisation makes the information clear and accessible and allows the user to drill down into the data. For example, you can see on the home screen a visualisation of how many sales agreements a company has. You can then review by sector, size, geography, language, and so on.' Luminance applies AI to unstructured data in multiple media and uses big data visualisation tools to present the findings in a clear and understandable way.

Luminance's plug-and-play model means it is accessible to businesses generally – and is not limited to big organisations that have the resources to invest in AI technology. It also requires minimal training, and training is frequently the barrier to any technology adoption. Users simply log in, upload the documents, and run the process. This supports the use case for Luminance for businesses involved in the occasional relatively small deal as well as large corporations handling multiple deals simultaneously.

Slaughter and May, Luminance's first law firm client, collaborated on the product's design, training it to 'think like a lawyer'. The firm is using Luminance for M&A due diligence as well as general compliance and regulation.

Senior partner Steve Cooke, who led the pilot project for Slaughter and May, ran the system in parallel with traditional document review, and confirmed that Luminance halved the time previously taken to conduct the same work. He told *Legal Week* that the system would be helpful for junior lawyers, allowing them to focus on more interesting work. 'It gives them their lives back. A lot of the due diligence work is not the most exciting work for lawyers.'[1]

In terms of compliance and regulation, Slaughters plans to use Luminance to manage Brexit-related changes. 'When we know what Brexit is, we will need to check every contract to make sure it is compliant', observed a partner. 'That will be infinitely easier with Luminance.'

Narrow AI as a service

Brexit has proved to be a good opportunity for legal AI to demonstrate its value because it is a single decision that will have specific implications for law and business. On the vendor side, NextLaw Labs has been working with RAVN to build an AI-powered app to analyse clients' exposure in relation to Brexit-related changes.

Firms are also developing their own bespoke applications around Brexit. In November 2016, Pinsent Masons announced the roll-out of an AI-powered commercial contracts solution to help clients identify Brexit-related risks in their existing portfolios, future contracts, and supply chains. The three-step tool uses the firm's AI platform, TermFrame (developed in-house), to extract, review, and analyse contract risks and produce actionable reports.

RAVN is expanding its range of specifically targeted applications, which include robots that handle banking regulations and legal professional privilege. These make legal and regulatory compliance faster and more reliable.

In 2016 a number of new, stand-alone narrow legal AI offerings have emerged in the form of web-based tools that speed up specialist tasks involving elements of expertise and ambiguity. A well-established example is TrademarkNow, which was launched in Helsinki in 2012 and has since expanded into a successful international business handling trademark review and clearance. Co-founder Anna Ronkainen, who also teaches a university course in legal technology, explains that TrademarkNow – an online tool that works on a subscription model – takes the 'heavy cognitive lifting' out of trademark review and clearance by calculating how close trademarks are to each other and presenting the user with a percentage figure. The answer is not a clear-cut 'yes' or 'no'. Like Luminance, it cuts research time in half for its global corporate clients, branding agencies, and company naming consultants by identifying anomalies almost instantly.[2]

TrademarkNow is currently a subscription service, but it is developing a pay-per-search model in response to feedback from law firms and other professional services organisations whose use of the service depends on the nature of the work they are handling. For example, some matters might require a lot of trade mark searches while others may require fewer or none. So it makes more sense for firms that handle trademark work intermittently to pay for TrademarkNow when they need it and pass on the cost to the client, rather than to have an ongoing subscription.

Corporate legal drives AI as a service

Legal AI has been driven at least in part by client demand – and the fact that corporations are already using AI for various purposes, including document analysis and extraction. Berlin-based Leverton is a specialist narrow AI offering that extracts and analyses data in real estate and finance documents. Leverton applies deep learning technology to abstract data from documentation, using neural networks to decipher meaning and crystallise this into attributes. This makes data transparent by looking at attributes rather than wording – for example, what clauses in contracts mean rather than how they are phrased. Leverton clients upload documentation to the Leverton platform, abstract it using a cognitive engine, and validate it – some data may require validation by multiple parties, including external law firms – and create a report. Leverton's APIs interface with enterprise resource planning (ERP) solutions such as SAP.

Capturing attributes (meaning) rather than text produces the capability of creating abstracts in multiple languages without the need for translation. So, the core attributes of a contract written in German can be understood by a Spanish or Chinese party to a transaction, or replicated to become part of a new contract in French or Italian without the need for translation or interpretation. Therefore, Leverton is a valuable tool in terms of leveraging knowledge and expertise across a business.

Leverton's clients are mostly large US and other multinational corporations, although the platform is used by their legal advisers, who use and review the abstracts that are produced using the system. This has led to Leverton working with law firms who handle multinational transactions – notably Clifford Chance, Freshfields, and Linklaters who are evaluating it for their own use.

As well as supporting knowledge-sharing across the business, as CEO Emilio Matthaei explained to AI Business, giving companies access to their core data without the need for translation or interpretation enables them to leverage it in practical ways – for faster, better-informed decision making, and process and efficiency improvements.[3]

Matthai explains why Leverton focuses sharply on finance and real estate, when it surely could be applicable to other areas: 'We aim to focus on doing specific things truly great, rather than everything just mediocre.' This is excellent news for the real estate sector, and leaves a gap in the market for similar products that cover other sectors with multinational players that could benefit from a similar approach to data transparency across languages and cultures.

Corporate legal departments are an important driver for developments in legal technology, not least legal AI, which has given rise to new ways of managing and delivering in-house legal services. Riverview Law's Kim – an intelligent platform for in-house legal services – blends BI and AI into a holistic AI-powered platform for managing in-house legal services. This is explored in more depth in the following chapter.

These products demonstrate the potential to extend legal AI beyond the Magic Circle and other large law firms that have the resources to invest in introducing and developing the technology. One of the challenges in broader AI adoption is that machine learning also involves machine teaching; self-service AI-powered services overcome this, making legal AI available to more law firms and corporate legal departments.

In a comprehensive article published on LinkedIn, consultant Peter Krakaur reiterates the first-mover advantage of AI adoption: 'Don't wait. AI is actively changing the way in-house professionals work, offering opportunities to deliver immediate value.'[4] Krakaur outlines multiple possibilities for in-house legal departments to deploy systems that include some element of AI: legal research, process automation, due diligence, e-discovery, contract analysis, legal spend analysis, expert systems, and legal outcome prediction.

Krakaur's recommendations for corporate legal departments appear to be narrower than Riverview Law or Neota Logic's offerings that are built on AI engines and other developments outlined in this book; nevertheless, they are important as they signify a fundamental shift in the legal services business model, driven by corporate decision making rather than legislative change such as liberalisation, or technological advances and other catalysts. This development is reflected by the fast take-up of pay-as-you-go resources, including Luminance and Leverton outlined above.

This leads to the realisation that, once you understand how AI works, it is just software. The off-the-shelf legal robots only hit the market in the second half of 2016, but as legal AI becomes commoditised and more affordable, it will no longer be a differentiator – unless it is bespoke or truly integrated into a firm's IT strategy and architecture. The following chapter looks at firms and corporate legal departments that are achieving this through (buying and building) the right blend of products and services, and the vendors that are collaborating with firms and each other to support an AI-first strategy.

References

1. Ward, A. '"It gives them their lives back" – Slaughters chief on what AI means for associates', *Legal Week*, 14 September 2016. Available at: www.legalweek.com/sites/legalweek/2016/09/14/ slaughters-strikes-deal-with-ai-technology-startup-luminance/?slre turn=20161011134624.
2. Anna Ronkainen's presentation at the Legal Geek conference in October 2016 explains how it works. See: www.slideshare.net/ronkaine/ ai-in-legal-practice-the-research-perspective.
3. 'Leverton enabling "More educated, faster and better decision-making" says CEO Emilio Matthaei', AI Business. Available at: Aibusiness.org/

leverton-enabling-more-educated-faster-and-better-decision-making-says-ceo-emilio-matthaei/#sthash.MVFMl0Qn.dpuf.

4. Krakaur, P. 'Artificial Intelligence (AI) in law departments: Opportunities', 5 October 2016. See: www.linkedin.com/pulse/artificial-intelligence-ai-law-departments-peter-krakaur.

Chapter 5:
AI first – Service as software

This chapter explores the concept of service as software as embodied by Viv – Siri co-creator Dag Kittlaus's virtual assistant that generates software in response to real-time natural language queries. Although legal AI has some way to go in that regard, the logical next step for trailblazers is building bespoke AI-powered applications that differentiate their services from those of their peers and competitors. This entails building on a versatile AI platform. We look at examples including Riverview Law's Kim, an intelligent platform for in-house legal services, and Neota Logic's expert platform for customer-facing applications, as well as firms with their own in-house developers creating tailored AI-powered services.

AI as a platform for legal services delivery reflects Google CEO Sundar Pichai's vision of 'an AI-first world' and the concept of 'service as software' (as opposed to software as a service) highlighted by Dr Harrick Vin at the AI Summit in London, in May 2016. The concept is digitally personified by Viv – Siri co-creator Dag Kittlaus's latest virtual assistant that generates software in response to real-time natural language queries. Viv uses sophisticated, cutting-edge technology, but the user experience (UX) is intuitive and feels 'natural'. AI as a platform is about user-friendly tools helping service delivery to excel against key performance indicators (KPIs).

AI as a platform – Riverview Law
The closest legal services offering to 'AI first' is Riverview Law's Kim. Kim was launched in December 2015 and its first two virtual assistants were rolled out in April 2016 in English and July 2016 in Spanish.

The Kim range of virtual assistants is used by Riverview Law's lawyers, who provide outsourced corporate legal services, and by in-house corporate legal departments to develop workflows directly from data, without the need for code. This differs from the due diligence engines which use machine learning to extract information from data but need to be programmed in the first place, or virtual assistants like ROSS, which are programmed to interrogate specific data sets. While these transactional support tools facilitate and accelerate routine functions, Kim is a platform for legal services delivery. Like ROSS, Kim is built on the IBM Watson platform. Riverview Law developed Kim in partnership with Professor Katie Atkinson and her computer science department at the University of Liverpool.

Riverview Law CEO Karl Chapman explains that Kim is available in three levels: basic, enterprise, and bespoke. In its basic form, Kim manages a legal team's workload, clarifying instruction requests so that work can be allocated quickly and appropriately. It provides the business with real-time management information about the volume and type of work the department is handling, which helps to guide and validate its strategy.

At enterprise level, organisations can configure Kim to their requirements. Chapman explains how it supports quicker and better decisions. 'A corporate lawyer could ask Kim to suggest the best order to renegotiate a series of contracts. It will produce a visualisation of all the contracts the organisation has with that client in terms of size, value, and risk for example, and suggest an order based on the variables you select. Or if there was a merger between two clients, you could ask it to present all your commercial arrangements with both of those clients, and how and why the terms and conditions may differ.'

Kim delivers relevant information to decision-makers instantly and suggests solutions in real time. Whereas, before, the legal team would have needed to find and review the contracts, and think about possible solutions, this is done automatically. 'Potentially Kim is also supporting non-lawyers involved in contractual decisions', adds Chapman. Like

LONald, Kim is cloud-based, although at enterprise level it can be installed on premises.

How does Kim work? CTO Richard Yawn, whose knowledge automation business CliXLEX was purchased by Riverview in 2015 and is part of Kim's core technology, describes Kim as 'an applied version of the theory of everything'. Kim uses 'contextual control' to create, automate, maintain, and evolve complex workflows and webforms without coding. So rather than ingesting content and using an AI engine to determine the context, Kim's algorithm assimilates the data, and then configures processes in response to the user's instructions (in the same way Viv does, but from its own data layer).

Kim doesn't infer context from large volumes of content in the same way as big data tools and AI-powered diligence engines. Rather it creates context from the inside out. The plus side is a straightforward UX to manage activity – templates, workflows, and work allocation – as well as risk and compliance. For example, one of Kim's key features is a triage process whereby it allocates incoming work to the appropriate resource – either in-house or to an external (panel) firm. Another major benefit is system agility – it is straightforward to configure and adjust templates, processes, and workflows in response to legislative and regulatory changes for example and its comprehensive reporting functionality.

The potential downside to Kim is that it takes time and resource to implement, particularly around establishing the data and context layers. Chapman and Yawn reiterate the importance of the underlying data layer. This relates back to business intelligence (BI) covered in Chapter 2 – you have to get the BI right in order to get the AI working effectively, because the AI engine is constantly drawing from, learning from, and updating the underlying data layer. Although Kim is effective across multiple devices, and assimilates multiple roles and perspectives, its effectiveness in driving desired behaviours (including compliance) depends on data accuracy and consistency across the underlying context layer.

Wavelength Law pares down the data-first approach to a concept that it has defined as 'legal engineering', using big data techniques including machine learning and data visualisation to generate sophisticated legal 'playbooks', capable of being understood by humans and machines, to capture and repurpose transactional information so that law firms and in-house legal departments can learn from each deal.

AI-powered apps – Neota Logic

The logical next step for AI first in legal is for trailblazing firms to move on from traditional IT development towards buying or building AI-powered applications and combining them into a bespoke platform that is a differentiator from peers in a competitive marketplace. This entails establishing a versatile AI platform and/or finding ways to integrate AI capability into existing and legacy systems. This area of legal AI is developing rapidly as more firms buy in to legal AI, and it signals what has been described as 'the end of the beginning' in legal AI. Consequently, this chapter is only scratching the surface as we look at examples ranging from customer-facing applications built on the Neota Logic platform to firms with in-house developers creating bespoke AI-powered services that are capable of supporting multiple tasks and processes.

Richard Seabrook, Neota Logic's managing director for Europe, said at the AI Summit that the 'last mile' to wholesale AI adoption is 'to include expertise in software'. Neota's smart apps tackle exactly that, encapsulating legal knowledge, reasoning, and judgement to provide self-service, real-time legal advice.

In common with Kim, the Neota Logic platform enables users to create AI-powered software without coding. However, unlike Kim, these can be stand-alone client-facing apps – meaning that a firm can create apps on demand. This is particularly useful for checking compliance. Taylor Wessing worked with Neota Logic to develop the 'TW: navigate PSC App', an interactive app that clients can use to find out whether they are subject to the People with Significant Control Rules (PSC). 'Clients can click on a link, and answer ten questions to find out immediately whether they are affected', explains Greg Wildisen, Neota's international managing director. 'Taylor Wessing's PSC App highlights the potential that intelligent software has to enhance the relationship between a law firm and its clients', commented Seabrook. 'Clients can quickly get a sense of how the rules may apply to their unique business situation, allowing for a more focused and valued relationship with their advisors.'

Another major advantage of this AI application is that it is infinitely scalable: 'Each app offers the ability to solve a particular problem for an unlimited number of parties concurrently.' This type of horizontal scalability – i.e. the ability to replicate a task multiple times simultaneously – is one of the key factors in transforming legal services, particularly when the task in hand involves specific expertise.

As a cloud-based platform, Neota also supports speedy developments such as applications conceived, built, and demonstrated at lawtech hackathons (see Chapter 7). It has also accelerated the start-up journey from concept to delivery (see Chapter 6), a recent example being AI Tech Support Ltd's Legal Intelligent Support Assistant (LISA). LISA is an AI commercial lawyer created by Adam Duthie of Duthie & Co LLP and legal futurist and entrepreneur Chrissie Lightfoot.[1]

AI collaboration

Reflecting the Partnership on AI formed by Google, Facebook, Amazon, IBM, and Microsoft announced on 28 September 2016, the legal sector has seen the beginnings of what is perhaps a vendor-led development: the growing collaboration between legal AI vendors and established legal IT providers, so that the new AI products integrate – or interface seamlessly – with legacy resources. For example, Neota Logic has developed strategic partnerships with RAVN and HighQ, a collaboration platform. A demonstration at the 2016 HighQ Forum showed how the three applications could be combined to automate specific legal processes. The demonstration used a fictional scenario involving the considerations and risks related to the potential purchase of shopping mall leases with multiple contracts. Information extracted from the data using RAVN's ACE software was used to populate HighQ iSheet columns, classifying it into different fields. Neota's technology worked on the extracted data to calculate values, assess the risk profile of each lease, and create a risk assessment report. If there are problems, these are identified and ranked red, amber, or green depending on the risk level. The entire process was conducted within the HighQ environment and all the data is presented clearly on the iSheet.[2] As Wildisen explained, the key elements were the ability to turn unstructured information into a structured format (RAVN) and then add in intelligent reasoning (Neota Logic) to ensure that the subsequent legal advice focused on the right documents.

Collaboration between AI vendors and legal IT providers is giving law firms more options, as they need to decide whether and where AI fits into their business. RAVN is one company that offers multiple channels and ways of applying AI, ranging from the bespoke services designed for BLP and others to pay-as-you-go resources, such as Extract Direct (described in the previous chapter). Kira Systems and ROSS offer the opportunity to create virtual assistants covering specialist areas of law, and train them to work with external and internal knowledge resources and interact across multiple practice areas and geographies, effectively extending the AI patchwork across the firm. The eventual goal could be to cover all practice areas; alternatively, AI could be deployed selectively to the parts of the business where there is a clear business case to do so.

Furthermore, driven perhaps by the realisation that mainstream AI can also be applied to legal, the legal sector is seeing increased integration between established legal IT providers and mainstream AI. For example, Thomson Reuters has announced that it is working with IBM Watson across multiple business sectors and its applied innovation group is introducing Amazon Alexa skills, so that legal customers who already use Alexa-enabled devices in their day-to-day lives can also have direct access to their Thomson Reuters Workspace. This type of development, which no doubt will be replicated by other legal IT vendors, will enable vendors to offer tech-savvy lawyers and clients a gateway into legal AI and the ability to extend agile working. It will also open up opportunities for firms to go beyond deploying AI in response to customer need, or in the interests of boosting the bottom line, and use it to leverage existing capabilities, and offer their clients new capabilities, by looking at what's already there that can be augmented with AI. This was discussed at ARK Group's 2016 KM Legal conference in New York, which considered ways of harnessing AI to support pricing, knowledge management, risk management, data security, and more.

A portfolio approach to legal AI

An increasing number of large firms are employing in-house developers to create tailored AI-powered systems. Pinsent Masons, Linklaters, and Freshfields Bruckhaus Deringer are among the growing number of firms creating bespoke combinations of (build-and-buy) products and services, which include AI. These trailblazing firms are building AI into their strategy going forward. This portfolio approach is a strategic way to create a sustainable differentiator, as off-the-shelf AI increasingly becomes the de facto tool for specific tasks. I should emphasise that these are just a few current examples to highlight a growing phenomenon. For the latest developments in law firm AI adoption, it is worth checking out Richard Tromans' *Artificial Lawyer* blog.[3]

Pinsent Masons was one of the first to develop its own AI-powered system. TermFrame was developed by Orlando Conetta, head of R&D, who has degrees in law and computer science, including a LLM in legal reasoning and AI. TermFrame takes a similar approach to Riverview's Kim in that its decision-making engine supports matter management by connecting lawyers with the knowledge and information they need at each stage in a transaction, i.e. it provides links to relevant templates, documents, and precedents.

TermFrame models the tasks and processes that lawyers perform, guiding lawyers through loan agreements and transactional work. 'It doesn't replace our matter inception software, but when there's work to be conducted, the lawyer answers a short series of questions and the system selects the appropriate framework (from a list of possible options). The framework may then ask further questions to classify itself further', says Conetta. 'The forms completed by the lawyer will be dependent on the type of work they are handling and the information they have entered in response to the questions. The system then presents the lawyer with the relevant forms and links to the firm's knowledge base.'

Like Riverview Law's Kim, TermFrame provides an assistance layer that understands the type of work being handled and provides relevant information at the right point in the transaction. Conetta explains that TermFrame does not look up precedents or legal information. The value proposition for the client, as well as for the firm, is in streamlining processes and making them more accurate by reducing human error, and providing the lawyer with the right information at the right time – and this tends to be the information that the client has provided. Again, the critical success factor is accurate and consistent data. David Halliwell, director of knowledge and innovation delivery, explains that because TermFrame is powered by a rules engine, it can be applied to any standardised process across the business, from project management to knowledge management. For example, it is also used to produce client-facing applications such as the Brexit risk solution featured in the previous chapter.

Another AI application developed in-house is Linklaters' Verifi, which checks client names for banks, and processes thousands of names overnight. This type of due diligence work is similar to BLP's LONald, powered by RAVN ACE and applied to real estate transactions (as featured in Chapter 3). Linklaters has moved on to a portfolio approach that combines its home-grown AI tools with external AI, working with RAVN, Kira Systems, and Leverton.

Strategically, Clifford Chance has taken a slightly different approach around productising its AI offerings. The firm purchased Kira Systems and (as explained in Chapter 3 by Bas Boris Visser, global head of innovation and business change), having trained it to work with Clifford Chance templates, processes, and precedents, the firm is white labelling it under their own brand so that they can productise it as a client service – i.e. they are offering Clifford Chance M&A due diligence as a service.

In November 2016, Clifford Chance announced that it was also collaborating with Neota Logic to develop an internal tool for assessing the impact of regulatory rule changes on financial institutions. As CIO Paul Greenwood explains, unlike an automated decision tree, the Neota system can process nuances and exceptions beyond a yes-or-no answer. 'For example, it will tell you whether you comply with certain regulations, and if you don't, what adjustments you need to make in order to achieve compliance.'

Freshfields too is using Kira Systems in its legal services centre to support transactional work across all its practice groups. As Isabel Parker, director of legal services innovation, explains, because Kira can be configured around the firm's custom provisions and knowledge base 'it complements our own legal expertise'. Together with information architect Milos Kresojevic, she is looking at different combinations of AI-powered tools, including Kira Systems and Leverton as part of the firm's commitment to innovation.

Kresojevic believes that AI has the potential to disrupt law firms, touching everything from routine processes to governance. 'It is not about buying or building a single system, but about how you combine different systems with information and legal expertise into an end-to-end system, as well as identifying potential new business opportunities.' In particular, he is looking at ways of productising the ability to deliver client-facing technology. Clients are looking at cost transparency, triage – ensuring their work is handled at the right level and at the right price – and operational efficiency – how to improve in-house legal processes. 'Including AI in end-to-end value creation is supporting the emergence of innovation as a key performance indicator and a differentiator.'

Although the Magic Circle and BigLaw are the obvious trail-blazers of legal AI, smaller firms are beginning to deploy it for specific purposes. London firm Hodge Jones & Allen worked with University College London to create an AI-powered prediction model to assess personal injury cases.

AI first in the legal sector is the ability to bring together AI elements with both legacy technology and other business technology. Experimenting with different technology – for example, combining virtual and augmented reality (VR and AR) with the capability of IBM Watson and other cognitive engines to power software that responds to natural language queries – offers more potential in terms of new ways to deliver legal advice.

The start-up dynamic is a key driver for legal AI, but in order to thrive, start-ups need investors to believe in their offerings enough to fund them. Perhaps a precursor to the portfolio approach was that until the second quarter of 2016, law firms seemed more willing to invest in legal AI than to deploy it. This trend has been accelerated by a rapidly expanding global lawtech start-up community, which is increasingly attracting the attention of mainstream investors. This and other elements of the global lawtech start-up phenomenon are explored in the following chapter.

References

1. See: Entrepreneurlawyer.co.uk/RobotLawyerLISA.
2. A video of the demonstration was published on YouTube. See: www.youtube.com/watch?v=oNEIxMSJOc4.
3. See: Artificiallawyer.com.

Part 3:
AI giving back – Return on investment

Chapter 6:
AI and lawtech start-ups

Legal AI is being accelerated by growing interest in investing in lawtech. This is has helped to create – and is driven by – the thriving global lawtech start-up community. Of course, lawtech start-ups are not limited to AI, but the first legal AI emerged from the start-up community, supported by investors that include law firms as well as the seed funding and angel funding that helps to get start-ups from concept to delivery – and hopefully to establish and expand into successful businesses. This chapter looks at who is creating and investing in emerging AI technologies.

Before the flood of AI take-up announcements in the second half of 2016, it seemed that more law firms were investing in AI and other lawtech start-ups than were actually using the technology. The fact that legal AI has turned a corner, and more firms are now actually using AI, is encouraging serial entrepreneurs and mainstream investors to get involved in the lawtech community.

AI's influence on investment in the legal sector is not limited to the start-up economy. It is also potentially shifting the law firm financial structure, particularly in liberalised legal services markets such as in the UK and Australia. The climate of investment in lawtech could well lead to investors looking to established law firms that are using AI-powered technology to extend their reach and develop new services. And law firms contemplating this type of expansion could attract external investors, or might consider partnering with (investing in) lawtech start-ups whose offerings could deliver on their strategy. As Giles Murphy commented in *Legal Week*,[1] with differentiation as the holy grail of professional services (and competitive advantage in any sector) 'underwriting almost all development plans is investment in technology'.

'While the Legal Services Act [2007, which allows non-law-yers to own and invest in law firms in England and Wales] has not had the impact that many expected, it is affecting the retail and commoditised end of the legal market, where hefty investment into IT systems can bring rewards. As artificial intelligence gradually improves, these trends will impact the whole legal market', adds Murphy, suggesting that this could mean that law firms will have to rethink their business and funding structure to include external investors.

As well as investing in AI-powered technology to automate volume work and repetitive processes, some law firms are involved in developing and backing game-changing technology. And a substantial group of forward-thinking law firms are positioning themselves as potential investors in lawtech start-ups, which are a significant force for change in legal technology and legal service delivery. There is much to gain; however, there are also challenges, which include choosing which start-up(s) will be the best fit for their firm and, increasingly, competing with mainstream investors who have a proven track record as seed funders, angel investors, and incubators.

The lawtech start-up phenomenon

2016 has been the year of the law tech start-up, fostered by well-organised regional meet-ups that bring together entre-preneurs and investors. There have long been entrepreneurs in legal technology – many of the high-profile technology businesses, consultancies, and publishers are, or started as, small (family) businesses. However, the past year has seen a marked acceleration in start-ups, and there is little doubt (among sensible observers, at least) that the next big thing in legal technology or legal transformation generally is likely to emerge from this movement, which continues to attract atten-tion and investment from the broader legal, technology, and investment community.

Leading legal IT commentator Bob Ambrogi has been maintaining a list of US and international start-ups. They are not dominated by AI companies but they demonstrate a growing trend. In considering how to define a start-up – i.e. when does a company stop being a start-up? – Ambrogi references two comments from *Forbes*. 'A company five years old can still be a start-up', observed Paul Graham, head of an accelerator called Y Combinator. 'Ten [years old] would start to be a stretch.' The same *Forbes* article quotes Warby Parker co-CEO Neil Blumenthal: 'A start-up is a company working to solve a problem where the solution is not obvious and success is not guaranteed.'

The latter point inspired Ambrogi to include some start-ups that are now closed, with a note of their status. 'The fact of the matter is that many start-ups fail', he wrote. 'An accurate picture of legal start-ups should include those that come and those that go, in my opinion.'[2]

This is equally true of AI lawtech start-ups, which have emerged from three main sources. The first, and most obvious, is legal technology companies such as RAVN and Luminance, which were founded by alumni of Autonomy (the UK's largest software business until its controversial sale to Hewlett-Packard in 2011). Autonomy's core technology was analysing large volumes of structured and unstructured data, so it was the perfect springboard for legal AI. Another source is law firms themselves, whose spin-off businesses include AI start-ups such as Thought River, incubated by Taylor Vinters, Dentons' Nextlaw Labs, which invested in ROSS, and Olswang's eqIP programme. The strongest supporters and incubators of lawtech start-ups are their global communities, which bring together entrepreneurs and investors. Promising start-ups and incubators are attracting mainstream funding from venture capital (VC) investors, notably London-based Balderton Capital.

Global communities

Jimmy Vestbirk set up Legal Geek to connect people and build a lawtech start-up community. He launched the Legal

Geek meet-ups in San Francisco with 30 attendees. The first London meet-up, held in May 2015, included a roundtable discussion and networking, and attracted 60 people. Legal Geek aims to make London the best place in the world to launch a lawtech start-up. The Legal Geek conference, held in London in October 2016, was the world's first lawtech start-up conference and it was attended by over 500 people from ten countries. In addition to the conference and start-up awards, Legal Geek's portfolio includes four meet-up groups: founders and innovators, women in lawtech, lawyers of the future, and disrupting legal industry. It has a charitable programme, Law for Good (featured in Chapter 7), and an incubator space bringing together investors, techies, entre-preneurs, academics, and legal professionals to help start-ups build connections and grow their businesses.

As Vestbirk explains, Legal Geek has over 1,000 members and its composition is changing. The first 100 people were lawyers who had learned coding and were looking to develop their ideas into a business, but recent joiners include investors, board members, partners, and innovation directors – people who are looking to connect with tech entrepreneurs and potentially collaborate with them and/or invest in their businesses.

At the Legal Geek conference, David Curle, director of market intelligence at Thomson Reuters Legal, described the lawtech start-up movement as 'a global horizontal phenomenon'. He highlighted the diversity of the start-up landscape and the fragmented nature of legal technology, which is illustrated in a slide from his presentation showing a multiplicity of start-up logos (Figure 1). The slide also emphasised the important role of academic centres such as CodeX at Stanford, which has focused on AI start-ups; informal meet-up groups such as Legal Hackers; and professional associations such as the European Legal Technology Association (ELTA), a community focusing on the European region, which was established in September 2016. Although this covers legal technology and innovation generally, AI vendor Leverton is one of its founding entities.

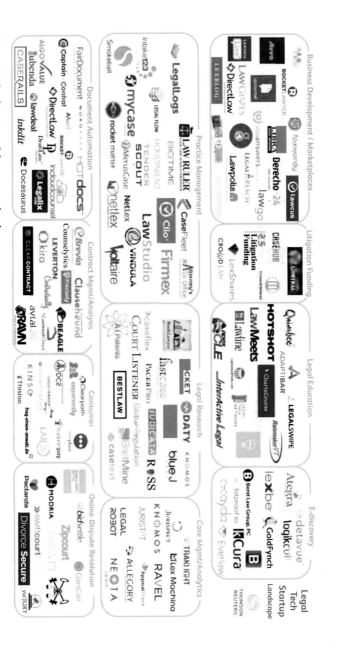

Figure 1: The diversity of the start-up landscape

Two of the major start-up hotspots that featured at Legal Geek are The Netherlands and Canada. The Dutch Legal Tech meet-ups and awards, which focus on the start-up community and its founders, are produced by Jeroen Zweers and Jelle van Veenan. Zweers is innovation director at Kennedy Van der Laan, a major law firm in Amsterdam, so the lawtech start-up movement in The Netherlands is connected to the mainstream legal community. Dutch Legal Tech involves an educational element – reaching out to law makers and law students – and its regular newsletter is distributed internationally.

Canada is also becoming a global centre for both lawtech start-ups and legal AI. Both ROSS and Kira Systems originated in Toronto, which is home to the Canadian LegalX Cluster, and legal innovation catalyst Law Made. Law Made is 'a global mobile pop-up for legal innovation', which was launched by Aron Solomon and Jason Moyse, based at the MaRS Discovery District incubator/accelerator. As well as driving and championing legal innovation and transformation within existing legal services businesses, Law Made, which is raising a $20 million start-up fund, offers entrepreneurs and start-ups hands-on support and advice.

The fact that tech start-ups are based on ideas rather than an iterative process means that they can incorporate the very latest technology straight away, and bypass legacy applications. This makes the start-up space a fantastic springboard for legal AI.

Investors and incubators

Not all lawtech start-ups involve AI, but AI is a significant component in the start-up phenomenon – partly because the technology is new and has been proved effective in narrow/ stand-alone applications and entrepreneurs are finding new ways of applying it. In the run-up to the Legal Geek conference, Legal Geek and Thomson Reuters created a map of the London lawtech start-up ecosystem (Figure 2). The yellow line shows start-ups based on machine learning, and the green dots feature cognitive computing, but AI also features in many applications

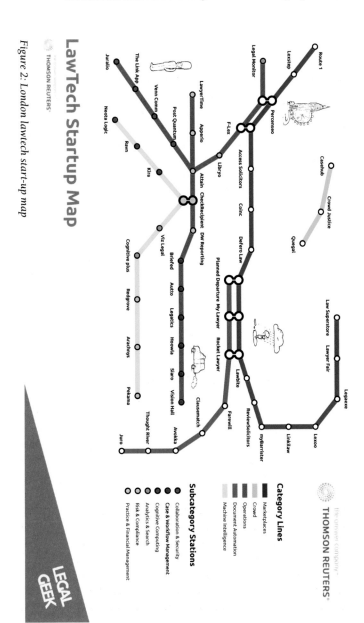

Figure 2: London lawtech start-up map

– notably on the (green) document automation line and the (red) operations line. For example, Autto offers intelligent workflow automation.

Leveraging AI platforms

Another catalyst for legal AI start-ups is the availability and usability of AI platforms. Entrepreneurs who are not AI technologists can build on existing AI technology, dramatically reducing development time and cost. Lawtech start-ups are also about creating brand-new services on existing platforms.

For example, Neota Logic (featured in Chapter 5) enables entrepreneurs to create new AI-powered applications without having to build the underlying AI engine. The latest example of this is AI Tech Support's Legal Intelligence Support Assistant (LISA), developed by CEO and legal futurist and author Chrissie Lightfoot in partnership with Adam Duthie of Duthie & Co LLP, and built on Neota Logic's AI platform.[3] LISA is described as an 'AI lawyer' that can advise both sides of a legal matter at the same time! LISA offers free trials of its impartial non-disclosure agreements (NDAs) and there are plans to extend the service to other commercial agreements.

Other legal AI start-ups use general-purpose AI engines to deliver specific outcomes. Joshua Browder's DoNotPay chatbot uses IBM Watson's Conversation service to gather information from users (who would otherwise need to fill in a lengthy form). Watson's Conversation[4] enables you to 'add a natural language interface to your application to automate interactions with your end users. Common applications include virtual agents and chatbots that can integrate and communicate on any channel or device. Watson Conversation combines cognitive techniques to help you build and train a bot.'

Partnering with law firms

Although advances in technology, a dynamic and supportive global start-up community, and interest from investors are driving legal AI forward, a major challenge for independent legal AI start-ups is the law firm procurement process, which tends to take a long time because of multiple approval layers and cultural considerations – lawyers are often reluctant to adopt new technology and require evidence that a new system is more effective than what they are already doing. And a new business needs to make sales within a certain timescale in order to remain viable. For example, RAVN's ACE only saw more general take-up among law firms after BLP's LONald was featured in the mainstream press and started winning awards. RAVN's experience highlights effective marketing as a critical success factor for legal AI start-ups, as well as a funding model that takes into account a longer delay than other industries before early adopters 'go public'.

One way of bypassing the law firm procurement process is to involve a law firm in the business as an investor or in a collaborative partnership. This potential win-win gives the start-up/ entrepreneur financial and practical support, and allows lawyers to develop and test prototypes. The benefit to the firm is the ability to harness the start-up dynamic and introduce some genuine innovation – which law firms and their clients consider an important source of competitive advantage. The critical success factor is that the process makes a real difference and addresses a genuine pain point.

Other firms have collaborated with developers to create their own legal AI products. This is generally the prerogative of larger firms that have the resources to support innovative new businesses, or spin-off businesses that are focused on innovation, such as DWF's 15squared.

It is quite unusual that a mid-market firm supports its own home-grown innovator. Taylor Vinters, a UK mid-market firm based in the Cambridge tech-cluster, is an exception. The firm acted as incubator for ThoughtRiver, which applies risk evaluation contract management in a way that supports compliance and decision making. It was founded in 2011 by Taylor Vinters partner Tim Pullan, who combines his work as a lawyer with running the start-up.

Although Taylor Vinters has a minority stake and provides financial, strategic, and practical support, ThoughtRiver is run independently and has the freedom to contract with other law firms and corporate legal departments that are not clients of the firm. This gives it the potential for significant growth. Taylor Vinters' chief executive Matt Meyer sits on the ThoughtRiver board: 'Collaboration is the best way for a mid-market firm to tap into innovation and the incubation model gives us the best of both worlds. We have access to innovative thinking and technology, and by embedding it in our organisation, our lawyers get to apply it on a daily basis and help to transform the legal services delivery model.'

Involving the angels

Lawtech meet-ups also attract VC funding. One such example is Balderton Capital. 'Law looks like a large pile of money where not a lot has changed', observed Balderton partner Suranga Chandratillake, who is founder of blinkx and former US chief technology officer at Autonomy.

Balderton backed TrademarkNow, one of the best recognised and longest standing lawtech start-ups. Co-founder Anna Ronkainen, who combines running a successful start-up with teaching a university course in legal technology, explained at the Legal Geek conference in London that TrademarkNow was one of the first lawtech start-ups in Europe to raise external funding. Founded in 2012, its seed investor was in Finland; angel investor, Balderton Capital, enabled it to expand into a successful international business with offices in London, Luxembourg, Ireland, and the US.

Start-up tips from TrademarkNow

Following her presentation at the Legal Geek conference, I asked Ronkainen for some advice for start-ups seeking VC funding. Here's what she had to say:

- Make sure your idea is solving a real problem. 'I advise

law students to gain work experience in a law firm or a start-up and learn from other people's mistakes.'

- Once you have an idea, connections are very important, particularly for seed funding, so keep networking.
- Ideas are overrated and execution is what counts. If the idea isn't perfect, you can tweak it later.
- Focus on creating a viable prototype, rather than a perfect pitch. Don't expect to get funding based on a PowerPoint presentation.

Balderton is looking for more opportunities in legal, and Chandratillake is particularly interested in working with teams that include lawyers as well as technologists – people with first-hand experience of the issues they are looking to address.

Other mainstream funders are already connected with legal technology, and the academic institutions that work on legal AI. For example, Autonomy founder Mike Lynch's Innovate Capital backs Luminance and several other AI-related start-ups (notably Darktrace) emanating from academia and the Cambridge tech cluster.

When it comes to law firms acting as angel funders, global firm Dentons was the first mover, launching innovation plat-form and business accelerator NextLaw Labs in May 2015. Its first investment was sophisticated, AI-powered virtual assistant ROSS Intelligence (featured in Chapter 3), which was estab-lished in a basement in Toronto by former lawyer Andrew Arruda with Jimoh Ovbiagele and Pargles Dall'Oglio from the computer science department at the University of Toronto. ROSS was supported by Y-Combinator before NextLaw Labs helped it to expand, both internationally and in terms of devel-oping the product.

Successful start-ups, including TrademarkNow, often benefit from seed funding and guidance before involving angel investors to help them to expand internationally. So, another challenge for lawtech start-ups is having to pause development to engage in additional funding rounds.

Seedcamp is a global first-round fund that has been investing in European pre-seed and seed stage start-ups since 2007. It recently moved into lawtech, and one of the start-ups it has invested in is Juro, whose AI-powered contract automation platform incorporates data analysis and a blockchain e-signature solution.

Another Seedcamp legal AI investment is US-based start-up Legit Patents, which applies a similar concept to TrademarkNow, applying natural language processing to the patent filing process to cover the initial searches, which are traditionally conducted manually by patent attorneys (patents include design concepts, so a keyword search is inadequate). Inventors can use an interactive bot to produce a definition of their inventions for the purpose of patent applications.[5] The fact that Legit Patents is also supported by Y-Combinator and Fantastic Ventures demonstrates the growing interest of mainstream investors in lawtech, and specifically legal AI.

NextLaw Labs is involved in multiple lawtech start-ups, not all of which involve AI. Its latest venture involves working as a co-investor with Seedcamp, to support software as a service (SaaS) legal compliance platform Libryo, and real-time contract automation and management platform Clause. In this way, NextLaw Labs and Seedcamp have facilitated the progression from seed funding to angel funding, enabling successful start-ups to ride the wave and expand without having to (temporarily) shift focus from product development to fundraising.

As Seedcamp investment manager and former corporate lawyer Tom Wilson explains, Seedcamp's partnership with NextLaw Labs gives lawtech start-ups the opportunity to take on co-investment that also opens doors to corporate relationships through Dentons' global network. It also allows start-ups to combine Dentons' sector expertise with Seedcamp's experience in incubating tech start-ups and helping them to expand.

Wilson's experience as a lawyer means that he has direct personal experience of the pain points that lawtech start-ups are seeking to address. He sees additional potential in applying

AI and natural language processing to contract automation and review, data analysis, and legal research. He sees more opportunities to leverage platforms like IBM Watson, and to build practical solutions such as Juro and Apperio (which deals with billing). He sees lawtech start-ups as 'a maturing ecosystem which will impact the legal market' and legal AI as an 'emerging toolset that presents smart founders with opportunities to build market-defining companies'. He adds that the legal services industry is one of the few remaining 'influential and lucrative markets' that stands to benefit significantly from emerging technology.

Start-up tips from Seedcamp

Wilson offers some advice for lawtech start-ups from the investor perspective:

- In areas where there are multiple offerings, like due diligence and legal research, data will be the differentiator – having access to more and better data will be a critical success factor.

- Choose your investors carefully. For example, if a corporate or a law firm is looking to invest at an early stage, consider what motivates them. Are they looking to use the product for their own competitive advantage rather than to be part of an industry game-changer?

Wilson adds that it will be interesting to see whether law firms act as incubators, like NextLaw Labs and Taylor Vinters, or whether they will look to buy start-ups or license and white label them to improve their own internal processes and branded client offerings, as Clifford Chance and others are doing.

Riding the wave

The burgeoning lawtech start-up community is no doubt a catalyst to shifting the business model and the purchasing patterns in legal IT – adding a new dynamic – but established players in legal and lawtech still have an important part to play. The fact that the Legal Geek conference in London was sponsored by The Law Society, Freshfields Bruckhaus Deringer, and Thomson Reuters demonstrates that the establishment is riding the wave of change. The Law Society sees the start-up community as intrinsic to its membership; Magic Circle and BigLaw are looking at harnessing not just new technology, but also innovation; and the big technology players are looking potentially to buy into the latest tools that will bring them and their clients new ways to deliver legal services, and new services to deliver. What it really signifies is that the 'new normal' in legal has moved from disruption to innovation. As serial entrepreneur Aron Solomon said, when it comes to lawtech start-ups, if you get on the wave early you can ride it for a long time.

It should not be forgotten that AI is a technology where it pays to be an early adopter – its core technologies, machine learning and natural language processing, mean that AI systems learn by doing, as well as by being taught. It follows, therefore, that as a system handles more data, it becomes more accurate and requires less human intervention (although, as the Microsoft Tay debacle demonstrated, regular monitoring is an essential component of effective AI). ROSS and others have demonstrated that developing or investing in the right start-up is likely to produce long-term competitive advantage.

From an investor perspective, the legal AI market means looking at what's new and following trends, as well as identifying pain points where there is a gap in provision – for example there are already a lot of start-ups offering due diligence, contract review, and document automation – or an opportunity to create something new. The influx of mainstream investors into the lawtech start-up market may well bring opportunities to introduce/adapt solutions from other verticals into the legal sector, as well as bringing proven experience and previous success to support lawtech entrepreneurs and help them to develop their businesses.

Lawtech start-ups are changing customer expectations of legal service delivery and this is shifting the legal procurement model that often stands in their way. For example, the freemium model used by TrademarkNow, among others, helps subscription and pay-as-you-go offerings break into the marketplace.

Another positive outcome of the combination of AI's scalability and the start-up dynamic is the opportunity to deliver more for less. Chapter 7 looks at how AI is being used to support pro bono legal work and charities, and to extend access to justice.

References

1. Murphy, G. 'Financing the law firm of tomorrow: Why external funding is here to stay', 11 August 2016. Available at: www.legalweek.com/sites/legalweek/2016/08/11/financing-the-law-firm-of-tomorrow-why-external-funding-is-here-to-stay/?slreturn=20160715045210.

2. Ambrogi's regularly updated list can be found here: www.lawsitesblog.com/legal-tech-startups.

3. For more on LISA, see: Lisa.neotalogic.com/a/about.

4. For more on IBM Watson's Conversation service, see: www.ibm.com/watson/developercloud/conversation.html.

5. 'AI start-up "legit" to disrupt patent world, secures seedcamp funding', *Artificial Lawyer*, 25 November 2016. Available at: Artificiallawyer.com/2016/11/25ai-start-up-legit-to-disrupt-patent-world-secures-seedcamp-funding.

Chapter 7:
AI for good

This chapter explores some of the ways in which AI is already helping to broaden access to justice for people and businesses by giving those who cannot afford to consult a lawyer, or are unsure whether they need one, a way of accessing legal advice with little or no financial outlay. It also looks at examples of how this is shifting the legal business model and law firm culture. Is legal AI good for the legal services market? Although there is an argument that, in some cases, 'robots' appear to be replacing lawyers, they may also be expanding the legal services market by providing new ways for individuals and businesses to exercise and protect their legal rights, thereby developing more work opportunities for lawyers.

On 28 September 2016, five of the world's largest technology companies announced the launch of Partnership on AI – 'to benefit people and society'.[1] Facebook, Amazon, Google/ Deep Mind, IBM, and Microsoft created a self-funded group to conduct research and promote best practices. Partnership on AI set itself eight goals, the first of which was to 'ensure AI technologies benefit and empower as many people as possible'.

In addition to its goals, Partnership on AI's eight tenets were preceded by the following statement: 'We believe that artificial intelligence technologies hold great promise for raising the quality of people's lives and can be leveraged to help humanity address important global challenges such as climate change, food, inequality, health, and education.'

In his opening keynote speech at the AI Summit in San Francisco in September 2016, Steve Eglash – executive director of the Stanford University Data Science Initiative, Artificial Intelligence Lab, Secure Internet of Things Project, and Stanford

AI Lab-Toyota Center for Artificial Intelligence Research – highlighted the power of AI to address human problems, explaining how computer vision is being used to measure poverty using satellite images, and deep dive inference engines are helping to combat human trafficking. These are global examples of what Eglash describes as 'human-centred and contextual AI'.

Governments are increasingly recognising the potential benefits that AI can bring. On 12 October 2016, the White House Office of Science and Technology Policy (OSTP) published a report, 'Preparing for the Future of Artificial Intelligence',[2] which includes a section on applications of AI for public good. Its recommendations include encouraging private and public institutions 'to examine whether and how they can responsibly leverage AI and machine learning in ways that will benefit society' and 'the use of AI to address social challenges', potentially through an 'Open Data for AI' initiative.

Broadening access to legal services and access to justice represents a great opportunity for AI to have a social impact, and although it is early days for legal AI, entrepreneurs in this field are already helping to make a difference. This is demonstrated by effective AI-powered solutions emerging from legal hackathons.

Brainstorming for good

What is a hackathon? Essentially, it is an event where programmers collaborate on software projects. Typically, teams of programmers collaboratively code solutions from scratch, focusing on a specific problem, theme, or cause. Hackathons are about brainstorming and building a solution in a limited time, typically 24 hours or a weekend.

In March 2016, Legal Geek founder Jimmy Vestbirk organised Europe's first LawTech hackathon under Legal Geek's 'Law for Good' programme. The 24-hour session, held at Google Campus, London, produced a selection of AI-powered triage tools to help community law centres to get more done and drive access to justice in the face of reduced public funding.

The brief was to find solutions to help Hackney Community Law Centre (HCLC), which provides free legal advice to the local community. The winner was Fresh Innovate, a team from Freshfields Bruckhaus Deringer, one of just a few major law firms that participated in the event. Fresh Innovate created a comprehensive portal management system that was coded and built overnight and included an interactive website. In joint-second place were an AI-powered SMS virtual receptionist (which also linked to an existing online translation engine) and an SMS appointment reminder service.

Hackathons bring the latest technology, including AI, to pro bono causes and access to justice, together with the start-up dynamic and culture – meaning that the format can produce quick results for an important cause.

As well as broadening access to justice by making limited resources go further, the process of quickly producing focused, cost-effective solutions and the collaborative spirit are transferable to legal services generally.

'The hackathon brought together a mix of lawyers and technologists working together in teams', explains enterprise architect Milos Kresojevic who led the Fresh Innovate team. 'This is a potential model for the future delivery of legal services, not just for start-ups but for larger firms like Freshfields too, as it leverages different skills to create tangible value.' Kresojevic describes how his team's inspiration and discipline helped them maintain their energy and enthusiasm. 'We worked in a way that we call "nano agile"', he says. 'This is about delivering one functionality every three hours. We decided on the functionalities and the order of delivery at the start, and every 20 minutes we had a five-minute stand-up meeting to discuss any issues or challenges. We focused on keeping delivery on track throughout the hackathon.'

Kresojevic is convinced that AI's qualities – flexibility and scalability – mean that it can bring significant help to society with a relatively small investment of resources and human effort. For example, it can support homeless people, asylum seekers, and others who may have language or other issues that make it difficult for them to access the legal advice they require to get the support they need. 'AI is not just about machines taking on work. It is also about connecting us back to our humanity', he says. 'Participating in the hackathon brought Freshfields' team a realisation of how AI-powered technology can help integrate people back into society.'

Freshfields' participation in the hackathon was driven by Kresojevic's commitment to contributing to the social good, and his desire to bring a different ethos to the firm's internal innovation efforts. 'It's empowering to work on a shoestring and create something new without requiring big investments', he says, adding that winning the hackathon created a shock-wave through the firm. 'Sometimes you have to look outside [the firm] to get validation for innovation. The hackathon was a level playing field where the brand has no impact, so it was also about bringing authenticity back to the firm.' Having won the hackathon, Freshfields worked with HCLC to deliver the solution and get it up and running.

The second 'Law for Good' hackathon, held a few days in advance of the Legal Geek conference in October 2016, focused on extending access to justice to rural communities – and, again, it produced AI-powered applications. The winning entries, which offered solutions to housing problems, included Atticus, an interface between people in need of advice and advice providers, intelligent workflow platform Autto.IO, and chatbot Sue-legal.

Hackathons – notably the global Legal Hackers movement[3] – are increasingly producing AI-powered access-to-justice solutions. For example, third prize at Scotland's 'Tech4Justice' hackathon, organised by the Law Society of Scotland and Legal Hackers Scotland, was awarded to Team Chatomate for 'Julie', a chatbot designed to guide people through small claims cases. Invited speakers included Dennis Mortensen, founder of x.ai and creator of popular AI personal assistant Amy Ingram, who schedules meetings for you if you add her to your calendar.[4]

The hackathon results demonstrate the value of AI in terms of scalability and development speed. AI applications go further than straightforward documentation of repetitive volume work; they can also handle multiple cases simultaneously, and even impartially advise both sides of the same case! Natural language processing avoids the need for the client to fill out long, sometimes confusing, forms, and machine learning enables the software to continuously improve its accuracy.

Chatbots extend access to legal advice

AI chatbots are making legal services more accessible and affordable, with free and freemium services chipping away at traditional legal business in a way that could reshape the industry.

DoNotPay – Rights and responsibilities

Stanford University student Joshua Browder's chatbot illustrates how technology can broaden access to legal advice in a way that enables people to exercise their legal rights without (necessarily) consulting a lawyer. This helps individuals seeking support or restitution, but it also protects society from public sector institutions, private sector organisations, and individuals exploiting areas of the law where it does not make financial sense for individuals to challenge unfair penalties or unfulfilled legal obligations or responsibilities.

As described in Chapter 4, Browder's free chatbot DoNotPay has successfully challenged some 200,000 parking fines by applying rules and regulations to live queries, using IBM Watson's Conversation platform. Since its launch in 2015, Browder has expanded his website's fleet of 'robot lawyers' to tackle homelessness, asylum claims, and landlord repairs.

Not only is the service completely free, but the bot will write a letter designed to maximise the applicant's chances of success by focusing on the most pertinent points, and can even help overcome language barriers. For example, in the case of Syrian asylum seekers applying for refugee status, the bot answers questions in Arabic, but produces documents in English.

Browder's next project is a free tool to enable law firms to build their own chatbots. He is also creating bots for legal-focused charities, including UK homelessness charity Shelter. He is already working with US law firms and anticipates a similar level of interest from UK legal services providers.

Although these bots provide access to free legal advice, are they replacing lawyers? The short answer is no. Browder has deliberately focused on areas where it would not be worthwhile or cost-effective for most people to consult a lawyer. Rather than replacing lawyers, Browder's bots are extending access to the law, and helping to implement it by highlighting legal obligations and accountability. This is practical altruism because it enables people to exercise their legal rights without prohibitive financial outlay.

LawBot – Is it a crime?

In October 2016, four Cambridge University law students – Ludwig Bull, Rebecca Agliolo, Nadia Abdul, and Jozef Maruscak – launched LawBot (see also Chapter 4). LawBot is a free AI-powered chatbot which extends the DoNotPay model to victims of crime. It uses natural language processing to determine whether a criminal offence has taken place. It covers 26 offences – including sex offences, injuries and assault, harassment, and property offences – some of which are straightforward (for example, burglary, theft, assault), while others are quite complex (such as abuse of a position of trust or psychological harm).

Like DoNotPay, the LawBot workflow takes you through a series of questions and, if it finds a match for an offence, it writes a letter that you can copy, edit where necessary, and send to the police or a lawyer to follow up the case. The dialogue is in natural language, and the artificial intelligence markup language (AIML) system understands natural language responses – for example, it acknowledges thanks, and it asks you to rephrase questions it doesn't understand. Likewise, the user can engage with LawBot and ask for definitions of terminology, and other clarification. Some of its questions are in multiple-choice format, but it understands and responds to natural language comments.

LISA – Taking care of business (agreements)

On a more commercial scale, AI Tech Support chatbot LISA is extending access to legal advice to entrepreneurs and small businesses that may not be able to afford to consult a lawyer. One of LISA's attributes is impartiality, which means that LISA can represent both sides of a case, where there would be a conflict of interests for a human lawyer or law firm. LISA will draft non-disclosure agreements (NDAs) for both sides in a deal, which would normally cost each party up to £500. AI Tech Support CEO (and legal futurist, author, and academic) Chrissie Lightfoot explained to *The Brief* that LISA is being offered free to encourage entrepreneurs and innovators to take legal advice when they might otherwise be deterred by a perception of prohibitive fees.[5]

Lightfoot reiterates that LISA is not designed to replace lawyers, because more complex agreements and legal problems will still need the human touch. Rather, this is about humans and machines working together to deliver better and more cost-effective legal services.

Replacing lawyers… or creating opportunities?

As AI is repeatedly referred to as the 'fourth industrial revolution', the legal and mainstream press continue to debate whether AI is 'good' for the legal industry – or whether (notwithstanding assurances from legal AI providers) it will eventually replace the need for lawyers. This is clearly not happening yet, but some lawyers fear that it is on the horizon, albeit any indications of this have so far been derived from science fiction rather than economics.

At the Legal Geek conference, Noah Waisberg, founder of Kira Systems, used the history of refrigeration as an analogy for legal AI. In the 1970s the average refrigerator required four times the amount of electricity as today's refrigerators do (although today they are, on average, 20 per cent bigger), but we still use more electricity for refrigeration because we keep more things cool.

Waisberg argues that the fact that Kira Systems can complete contract review in 20–60 per cent less time than it takes to complete the process manually will not necessarily mean that law firms will employ fewer associates. In fact, it may mean that businesses and individuals will purchase more legal services as they become faster to deliver and more affordable. Waisberg referenced Jevons' economic paradox that increasing the efficiency with which a resource is used tends to increase the rate of consumption of that resource, by increasing demand.

Waisberg believes that, as the regulatory environment continues to become more complex, the demand for legal services will increase, but demand will remain price dependent. 'Even huge companies will spend more on legal services if legal services are priced in a way that they feel offers value. So more legal work will depend on the price. For example, as the regulatory cost of being a public company increased due to [The] Sarbanes-Oxley [Act of 2002], there were fewer initial public offerings.' This follows the same principle as Browder's DoNotPay chatbot: more people are challenging parking tickets because it has become easy and affordable – and therefore worthwhile.

However, this remains to be seen. As Wright Hassall IT director Martyn Wells writes, the ready availability of free or freemium legal AI applications is likely to impact legal services IT provision as well as the legal services procurement model.[6]

Robot justice
Access to justice
AI's scalability and cost-effectiveness represents fantastic potential to extend access to justice generally. This has not been lost on forward-thinking legal educators. Professor Tanina Rostain, co-director of the Center for the Study of the Legal Profession at

Georgetown University Law Center, teaches a 13-week course on Technology, Innovation, and Legal Practice that uses the Neota Logic AI-powered platform to develop pro bono apps. As the *ABA Journal* reported,[7] the course is built around a competition among teams of three or four students developing apps that help make complex areas of the law generally accessible to those who need to understand and apply them. Student groups are partnered with participating government, not-for-profit, and charity organisations. These win-win projects are developing tech-savvy future lawyers and applying Neota Logic's expert system to promote access to justice.

Predicting case outcomes

A popular legal AI application is to predict case outcomes. Law firms Hodge Jones Allen, in London, and Bradford & Barthel, in San Francisco, both apply AI-powered predictive analytics to big data sets to analyse personal injury cases. The forecasts are used to inform decisions and advise clients on whether and how to progress similar cases. LexisNexis' Lex Machina uses multiple data points to predict case outcomes, and Premonition ranks lawyers by their success rates in particular cases.

AI developed by University College London, the University of Sheffield, and the University of Pennsylvania is predicting the outcomes of human rights trials to 79 per cent accuracy.[8] Researchers identified English language data sets and applied an AI algorithm to the text that could look at legal evidence and ethical issues. It found that European Court of Human Rights judges tended to look more at non-legal factors than strictly legal factors. Accurately predicting case outcomes could be considered the first step towards developing AI judgements – or robot judges.

AI judges?

One of LISA's key attributes is impartiality, and a logical progression would be AI judges that combine predictive analysis with AI-powered impartial decision making – but, so far, this type of technology has been discredited by latent biases in algorithms.

The UK government's £1-billion vision for the digital transformation of the justice system[9] takes a tentative step in this direction as it includes online dispute resolution (ODR), and the prospect of people being convicted online for minor offences such as TV licence evasion, as well as developing Lord Justice Briggs' recommendation for an online court. Although the proposals do not include AI, they have prompted discussions about 'AI judges'.

Science fiction has long predicted robot judges and automatic justice. For example, the 1989 film *Back to the Future 2* includes an efficient example from its vision of 2015 – imagined 30 years earlier – showing young criminals caught, tried, and convicted moments after they commit a crime. *Minority Report*, based on Philip K. Dick's dystopian short story that imagines a future legal system using 'precognition' to prevent crimes before they happen, is reflected in technology being developed in China that uses data to prepare for 'security events'.

When it comes to determinations and judgements, AI in law is complicated by ethical considerations. Because law is a set of rules and procedures, in theory, the entire judicial process should be ideal for intelligent automation. In practice, however, laws exist to govern human behaviour and form a framework for society, and as there are contextual variations around what society considers acceptable or unacceptable, and these also develop differently across different communities, it is debatable whether automating justice is appropriate or desirable.

Furthermore, while there is no doubt that extending access to justice by making legal advice more accessible and affordable benefits individuals and society generally, there are ethical concerns about taking automation too far. This is just one of the challenges and opportunities around robots in law that will be explored in the following chapter.

References

1. For more on this see: www.partnershiponai.org.
2. Office of Science and Technology Policy (OSTP), 'Preparing for the Future of Artificial Intelligence', 12 October 2016. Available at: www.whitehouse.gov/sites/default/files/whitehouse_files/microsites/ostp/NSTC/preparing_for_the_future_of_ai.pdf.
3. See Legalhackers.org.
4. See: X.ai/about.
5. Gibb, F. and Ames, J. 'March of the legal bots continues', *The Brief*, 21 November 2016. Available at: Nuk-tnl-deck-email.s3.amazonaws.com/11/03b2ceb73723f8b53cd533e4fba898ee.html
6. Wells, M. 'What AI is really going to do to the legal industry', 22 November 2016. Available at: www.linkedin.com/pulse/what-ai-really-going-do-legal-industry-martyn-wells.
7. Carter, T. 'Professor Tanina Rostain has her students developing access-to-justice apps', *ABA Journal*, 23 September 2015. Available at: www.abajournal.com/legalrebels/article/tanina_rostain_profile.
8. As reported on the UCL website: www.ucl.ac.uk/news/news-articles/1016/241016-AI-predicts-outcomes-human-rights-trials.
9. Ministry of Justice and HM Courts and Tribunals Service, 'Transforming our justice system', September 2016. Available at: www.gov.uk/government/publications/transforming-our-justice-system-joint-statement.

Chapter 8:
AI challenges

This chapter looks at the key legal AI challenges. These include recognising AI's limitations – what it can and cannot do – as well as some of the practical and ethical considerations. We examine cultural issues around roles and work styles in law firms, as well as challenges to the business model, and look at how some firms and vendors are adopting strategies that are turning challenges into opportunities.

The previous chapter outlined some of the ways in which legal AI is being used to extend access to justice. These include chatbots that help individuals and businesses exercise their legal rights, such as DoNotPay, which handles legal challenges; LawBot, which supports victims of crime; and LISA, which produces NDAs.

Robot Lawyers Australia,[1] another chatbot, supports unrepresented defendants accused of a minor driving or criminal offence. It differs from the examples above in that it produces a document for presentation in court. Although the website states clearly that it is not a lawyer and that it is better to have a lawyer in court with you, if you can afford one, if the defendant does choose to present the document in court, the chatbot's output could affect the outcome of the case.

Legal, ethical, and regulatory considerations

Robot Lawyers Australia is just one example that raises ethical considerations about how the law should apply to legal AI, and whether AI needs its own regulation. Law firms are already considering how existing law could apply to robots, and how the law might have to change to regulate them. Although this is a legal challenge, rather than a practical one, the current and potential regulatory landscape around AI is also relevant to the practical application of legal AI.

For Robot Lawyers and other chatbots, the situation is quite clear. The party using the chatbot chooses whether or not to present the document to the court, send it to a local authority, or carefully review the details of LISA's NDA before signing it. But when it comes to due diligence, contract review, or legal research – who is responsible for a false positive or negative produced by the AI engine? I have sought some expert insights around responsibilities for the consequences of using AI.

AI – A regulatory dilemma

John Flood is Professor and Director of the Law Futures Centre at Griffith University in Queensland, Australia, Honorary Professor of Law at UCL, and Visiting Professor of Law at the University of Westminster. He has written extensively about how globalisation, technology, and other factors are changing the practice of law. Here is his opinion on AI, regulation, and legal education.

While it's doubtful any AI bot will pass the Turing test yet, AI is now an integral part of life, including the law, and many people will not realise they are communicating with a machine. Law has passed through a number of technological revolutions – pens, printing, computers – but they are essentially passive, reactive innovations. What happens when technology becomes active or autonomous?

The regulation of legal services is based on the human factor, that lawyers have a fiduciary duty to their clients. So, the labour component of legal services makes them expensive to produce, with the result that fewer people can afford lawyers. Moving from labour to capital improves returns and saves costs, hence the recognition that AI has a significant role to play. We see this actively pursued in NewLaw.

At the moment, legal regulators don't regulate AI or machines. This is based on the idea that humans are responsible and accountable for what machines do. Yet as legal services and the profession become more digital, they will rely on outsiders (e.g. IBM Watson) to deliver the service. There are problems here: how can you be accountable for something you don't understand? And as machines become more autonomous (self-learning), to what extent are humans culpable for the actions of machines? Is education ready and capable of teaching AI to new lawyers?

Legal doctrines like 'vicarious liability' will take care of some of these issues, but that line of accountability will thin out over time as machines become remote from their programmers. And who exactly will be accountable? IBM? The law firm? Or both? Regulators themselves will need to skill-up to take on these challenges. The ABA Commission on the Future of Legal Services is a step in the right direction.[2] It's reasonable to envisage hybrid law firms – part human and part machine – with potentially a degree of algorithmic control co-existing with human activity. Imagine if 'smart contracts' really do become smart!

With legal education, we haven't begun to consider these factors. A few innovative programmes such as Iron Tech Lawyer and Law Without Walls have so far failed to herald an educational revolution. But legal education, and its regulators, will have to adapt to the technological changes now being incorporated into law.

Paresh Kathrani is a senior law lecturer at the University of Westminster whose research covers legal adaptation. On regulating AI in the legal profession, he agrees with Professor Flood, emphasising the need to recognise that regulation is about people, not machines. 'The notion of regulation suggests an element of agency. We cannot regulate machines, but we can regulate the people who use them', he explains. Kathrani, too, believes that existing regulations on technology also cover legal AI. 'There is no difference between regulating a lawyer's use of a PC and regulating their use of an algorithm or AI engine. The existing codes and ethics are broad enough to cover artificial intelligence.'

Kathrani suggests that it is people's perceptions of AI that are creating some of the hype around it. 'When people envisage machines making autonomous decisions and potentially creating problems, they are separating the machine from the operator. The regulation issue is ontological – it's about how we classify AI.' This point is highly relevant to the current state of legal AI, which supports legal practice by finding the right information to assist lawyers or individuals with a legal issue. 'It is about who takes responsibility for the outcome. At the moment, an individual has to press a key to create and send a document, so the end point lies with the human operator.'

'Law is a human endeavour, but adaptation is crucial', says Kathrani. 'Law doesn't exist in a vacuum. It has to evolve with the changes that are taking place around it. We need to strike a balance between humanity and justice and ensure that intelligent machines are utilised in an effective manner.'

Risk and liability

Another challenge involves the notion of legal risk. 'The client is always human, as law is a human endeavour', says Kathrani. 'By choosing a chatbot instead of a human lawyer, that client is assuming an element of risk. However, if a client consults a human lawyer, some element of risk could be apportioned to the lawyer, who might advise one course of action over another. The risk that people are prepared to assume depends on the context, and if something goes wrong due to a glitch in a machine, the legal risk may transfer to the person who designed [or taught] the machine.' This observation emphasises the need for monitoring and approvals to be built in to machine learning systems to ensure that they remain accurate.

When it comes to legal and business risk analysis and management, legal AI comes into its own. Diligence engines such as Luminance, RAVN ACE, and contract comparison products such as Kira Systems help firms and legal departments to manage risk by flagging up anomalies that could compromise a deal or the outcome of litigation. Virtual assistants such as ROSS and Riverview Law's Kim ensure that knowledge and precedents are applied comprehensively – although, ultimately, their accuracy depends on the quality of the data they are querying. There are also narrow AI applications designed to address and manage specific risks. For example, ThoughtRiver applies risk evaluation to contract management in a way that supports compliance and decision making, and Juro builds in blockchain and e-signatures to automated contract generation.

Kathrani believes that as cases become more complex, or the risk becomes more significant or business critical, the risk profile shifts, and whether to use AI becomes a strategic and potentially a moral consideration. This in particular would start to apply to a more generalised use of AI to support decisions around legal advice, and ultimately even judgements.

However, risk and liability can also represent a limiting factor for AI, observes Andrew Joint, technology partner at Kemp Little, because certain activities are only legitimate if they are carried out by a qualified lawyer. However, the list of reserved activities is relatively limited. There are also liability issues around the use of AI – the choice of methodology to carry out data extraction for M&A diligence, for example, does not remove responsibility from the lawyer handling the case. 'I cannot imagine a scenario where automating one or more elements of my job would remove my liability if something went wrong', adds Joint. 'It is akin to supervising the associates who work with me on a matter. It is supervision on escalation in that I don't need to check everything they do. So, if I use an AI tool instead, it does not remove my responsibility for the advice

I deliver or mean that the firm no longer has liability for the consequences, which is why [the firm] has to have professional indemnity insurance.' This is also why it is important for firms to have appropriate checks and balances, but this is also a challenge – because you cannot check everything the machine does (because the purpose of using AI is to process large volumes of data instantly) and the nature of machine learning – which enables it to improve its performance in terms of accuracy and quality – means that the operator loses control over the minutiae of the process, which some lawyers find unsettling.

Legal and regulatory compliance
Legal AI enables compliance with legal and professional rules and regulations to be built in to workflows and processes, eliminating human error from research, diligence, and contract review. Legal AI brings consistency, applying the same values simultaneously across high volumes of structured and unstructured data. Diligence engines which actually 'read' and understand documents can identify anomalies, including pages missing from documents and relevant information from images, so they are more thorough than human review. Because they can read multiple documents simultaneously, unlike a human being, their document analysis is more accurate.

However, like any automated system, AI systems can identify false positives (although machine learning gradually minimises this) so it is necessary to make sure the machine is learning from and applying the right precedents to legal research and transactional work. This means processes need to have built-in monitoring and approvals to ensure that they remain accurate and compliant. Lawyers are still needed to check the output and make sure that the machines are learning from the right data. But even with human monitoring and approvals, because legal AI reads multiple documents concurrently, it will still be many times faster than completing the processes manually. Compliance can be built in to AI-powered workflows such as Riverview Law's Kim, which creates scalable compliance processes across matters, practice areas, or across the business.

Legal AI's strength as a point solution makes it ideal for regulatory compliance. AI platforms enable firms to build solutions for managing compliance with specific regulations. Some vendors have developed solutions to address compliance issues affecting particular sectors. For example, RAVN ACE is used to extract International Swaps and Derivative Association (ISDA) data from contracts in line with banking regulations.[3]

Another approach is for firms to use an AI platform to create client resources. Taylor Wessing's 'navigate PSC', built on Neota Logic, is an interactive app that clients can use to find out whether they are subject to the People with Significant Control rules. 'Clients can click on a link and answer ten questions to find out immediately whether they are affected', explains Neota's Greg Wildisen, adding that a major benefit is the ability to advise an unlimited number of parties concurrently.

Other firms have created client-facing solutions to industry-related compliance issues from scratch. At Linklaters, information architect Ben Gardner and his team used open-source software to create Verifi, an AI solution which checks client names for banks in a fraction of the time it takes to do the same task manually.

Implementation challenges

It is also important to look at AI from the legal practice perspective, particularly as more law firms are establishing specialist practice groups to advise clients on the legal aspects of AI.

Legal AI is not a one-size-fits-all solution

The first consideration is that, notwithstanding all the talk about legal AI, it is not a one-size-fits-all solution and it is not applicable to all legal services or all aspects of legal services. Like big data, it is most effective in the volume space, once the initial investment of time and money has been made, in terms of data extraction and contract management and assembly.

Virtual assistants like RAVN, Kira Systems, and ROSS save transactional lawyers time and make their services more cost-effective.

For in-house legal departments, there is the holistic option of Riverview Law's Kim, subscription and on-demand services such as Luminance and Leverton that fulfil specific functions, as well as more specialist services that deal with particular specialisms such as TrademarkNow. The value-add of all these services is they reduce the time it takes to complete essential routine tasks and, as clients become increasingly aware of this, AI will become part of panel RFPs (just as use of technology is now, for example in respect of e-billing, collaboration tools, and more recently data analytics), and these systems will become widely used.

It is, however, important to recognise that AI is not applicable to all matters; for example, not all matters involve large volumes of documents, or can re-use multiple clauses from previous cases. They may be based on human factors, or the best way forward may be negotiation or mediation. Or they may be test cases which will become precedents later.

It is important to establish a use case for whether and how AI will bring improvements for the firm and its clients, because legal AI that is not a straightforward, on-demand subscription or pay-as-you-go service requires a significant and ongoing commitment: to training the machine, to monitoring and maintaining the quality of the data it interrogates and its outputs, and to helping people transition to a different way of working. Because legal AI doesn't 'just happen'.

At Liverpool University, Professor Katie Atkinson identifies knowledge acquisition as a major challenge. 'Legal AI programmes take a long time to set up and, unless it is a very narrow use case, legal AI is not a one-size-fits-all solution', she says, identifying issues of trust and integration with legacy systems as common barriers to implementation.

'People see the magic and think it will be automatic, but it's not', says Derek Southall, partner and head of innovation and digital at Gowling WLG. Derek worked with IBM Watson to develop a proof of concept for a project using Companies House data, which is publicly accessible but not specifically searchable. 'Challenges included getting the right corpus, managing multiple formats, and addressing data protection issues – but we got there in the end.'

Machine learning involves machine teaching

Initially, legal AI systems needed to be configured to individual firm and practice area requirements. Products like RAVN ACE, ROSS, and Kira Systems receive initial 'machine teaching' from the supplier, and the machine learning continues as the firm adds in its own data and processes. It can then be offered to the client as a branded product, either within the organisation or as a client service.

But machine teaching is a barrier to adoption as it takes time and resources. Bas Boris Visser at Clifford Chance identifies the following implementation challenges:

* Training the machine;

* Training lawyers to use it; and

* The lawyer mindset.

'Don't underestimate cynical lawyers – they won't accept it until they see evidence that it works', says Visser.

To some extent, this challenge is addressed by self-service products like RAVN Extract, Luminance, and Leverton, as well as specialist resources like TrademarkNow and Legit Patents,[4] which broaden the appeal of legal AI but reduce its ability to bring competitive advantage as they can be accessed by anyone, on demand. This type of legal AI will no doubt become the usual modus operandi for certain types of work, and will drive costs down.

A related issue that has been identified is the impact on training of junior lawyers who start their training by undertaking simple, repetitive tasks with the idea that if you look at enough contracts, you will get to know them! The counter-argument is that rather than deploying highly qualified people to carry out undemanding work, AI will free them up to spend more time with their mentors and peers on value-added tasks and training.

Disrupting the law firm value chain

AI-powered innovation is disrupting the law firm value chain. For example, AI-powered due diligence means that the Magic Circle and BigLaw firms will not be able to charge their clients for this element of their work in the way they previously did. Ron Dolin, senior research fellow at the Harvard School of Law's Center on the Legal Profession, told CNBC: 'These firms are looking at future doom if they don't start playing with business models in different ways.'[5] As more law firms replace first-year associates with legal AI for routine tasks (and deploy them in other roles) law firms will no longer be able to bill for the time it takes to conduct due diligence and other routine tasks. 'This is not reversible', he added. 'The first-year associate as cash cow to partnership is breaking.' This is true, and the billable hour is indeed under threat, but this is not as dramatic as it sounds, particularly in relation to the UK's liberalised legal services market where fixed and capped fees are commonplace, and document automation has been around for a long time.

And while AI is not about to replace lawyers per se, it is encouraging corporate legal departments to in-source some of the work that used to go to external counsel. *Legal Week* reported that Vodafone Global Enterprises has doubled the size of its team and implemented Riverview Law's Kim for contract management with the idea of using Kim 'across Vodafone's markets for contracting activities'. Kevin Gidney, chief technical officer at Seal Software, told *Legaltech News* that to stay competitive, law firms will have to turn to AI to increase productivity and efficiency.[6]

Martyn Wells at Wright Hassall adopts a somewhat pessimistic view of the cost-benefit implications of AI for mid-market firms, expressing concern that free and freemium AI-powered legal bots, and the fact that AI will make matters easier to predict, will drive down legal services pricing. Wells believes that 'AI pricing will need to drop like a stone tied to a heavy boulder in order to penetrate the smaller firms lower down the size league tables, unless of course these firms have been obliterated by the AI pricing dogfight. Lots of adoption and usage to come but at massively compressed margins once all those upfront sunk development and integration costs have been recouped from the lucky go-firster gang. At this point […] market predation factors will come into play; we might start seeing existing AI vendors become annexed by larger scale legal service providers.'[7]

Both Gidney and Wells discuss the potentially prohibitive cost to mid-market and smaller firms of adding AI to the legal technology mix. Potential ways to minimise this include the AaaS technologies that will provide scalability on demand, enabling smaller firms to take on matters which involve volume work without investing in buying or building AI technology (in the same way as cloud computing addressed storage issues). As legal AI becomes more affordable and accessible, it will no doubt drive prices down, but it will also open up market opportunities, as Waisberg, Lightfoot, and others envisage.

Furthermore, AI technology is already here and several major suppliers are offering their AI technologies on trial, discounted, or freemium models, and are making open source platforms and software available to developers, so it may be worth firms who are considering introducing these technologies experimenting with what they can bring to their businesses before making any commitment or significant investment.

Strategic choices

Because legal AI is fragmented, law firms and legal departments need to make strategic choices around whether AI is right for them, and which solution or combination of solutions fits their business and the type of work they handle. Another challenge is deciding the right kind of AI for the job and whether to build or buy. This would depend on the firm's budget versus its ability to commit resources to developing a system in-house and making it work (as Pinsent Masons has done with TermFrame).

Generally speaking, cost – in terms of time and money – is a significant barrier. As Richard Hodkinson, CTO at DWF, and Derek Southall at Gowlings, observe, configurable systems such as IBM Watson are prohibitively costly for law firms in terms of expenditure and set-up time. This is where building in-house AI comes into its own. Ben Gardner at Linklaters uses open source technology to develop solutions that match the requirements of particular groups of clients. The Verifi tool for financial services organisations is a case in point.

Because legal AI is so far narrow and the market is immature, a firm can't simply invest in an AI system that covers all of its requirements, or follow the legal IT procurement model and buy one of the two or three most popular systems. It needs to choose the right one. So, a key strategic challenge is bringing together multiple elements into a holistic legal AI architecture. Thus far, only a few firms are achieving this. Examples include Freshfields, which is combining Kira Systems' contract analysis for M&A due diligence, Neota Logic for multijurisdictional filing, blockchain-enabled smart document generation for capital markets work, and semantic web technologies for universal searching; and Clifford Chance, which uses Neota Logic for compliance and Kira Systems for M&A due diligence.

Integration with existing systems is another challenge. Vendors are recognising that integration presents a potentially serious barrier to adoption and are working collaboratively to address this. Neota Logic and RAVN integrate with other systems – and each other. At Clifford Chance, Paul Greenwood recognises the potential to bring together multiple narrow legal AI solutions into a bespoke AI-powered system.

Governance and new roles
IT governance is a strategic consideration, particularly as legal AI is changing some roles within law firms and creating others. For example, decisions need to be made around machine learning.

Who is teaching the machine? Who should be monitoring the outcomes, and what comparisons need to be made? Mike Nolan, IT director at BLP, highlights that the pace of change means firms require different skillsets. 'We need to match the skillsets in our business to its strategic priorities and technology needs', he says. Whereas firms have employed business analysts for some time, more firms are now recruiting data scientists.

Using AI to automate some legal support processes is changing roles within law firms. For example, as more firms employ ROSS for legal research, legal knowledge roles will change from carrying out research (which will now be conducted by ROSS) to ensuring the necessary material is available for a machine to access, and monitoring and training the machine to produce the most accurate, valid, and appropriate results. Roles related to maintaining data quality are moving up the value chain as the quality and accuracy of the output of AI systems depends on it working with the broadest possible range of high-quality data. It doesn't have to be in a particular format, but it needs to be valid, relevant, up-to-date, and most importantly, accessible.

Data as a critical success factor has also produced brand new roles. A case in point is the legal engineer, which is defined by Drew Winlaw (who is himself a legal engineer!) at Wavelength Law as follows:

Legal engineer
(UK /ˈliː.gəl en.dʒɪˈnɪər; US /ˈliː.gəl en.dʒɪˈnɪr/)[8]

noun – a person that sits at the interface of technology, law and data, and who is trained and skilled in the construction of designed legal solutions.

verb (used with object) – to navigate, connect and integrate point legal technical solutions with the real time practice of law.

Origin – English, early 21st century to mid-2016. A concept developed by a few enlightened individuals from Susskind to Winlaw.

Broadly, Winlaw applies design thinking to integrate AI and other technologies and processes that involve working with data to create a holistic approach to legal technology. He describes his role as follows: 'A lot of my work involves designing and implementing systems that reduce duplication and use sensible automation in the right part of the process. Systems need to interact with humans in a "polite" manner and help them achieve something more quickly or accurately with the system than without. Understanding data reliability, data cleansing and visualisations that mean something are all really important factors in great system design.'[9]

Building AI into law firm culture

The most important challenges to overcome are around culture. It seems that the lawyers themselves are quite accepting of machines replacing them to do repetitive, routine work they don't enjoy doing. Proponents of legal AI agree that automating routine tasks in a way that frees up lawyers to do more interesting and challenging work is culturally beneficial. Wendy Miller at BLP highlighted LONald's popularity with the real estate disputes group (see Chapter 3).

There are implications for law firm management structures and responsibilities. Replacing junior associates with AI does not change the partners' responsibilities around the delivery and outcome of the work; however, it removes the relationship element of supervising the diligence and legal research work that contribute significantly to the outcome of a commercial transaction or the intelligent contract generation software that sealed the deal. 'Because there is an element of trust between me and my team, I can rely on them to escalate anything they are not entirely confident about. How can I be assured of that comfort from a machine?' asks Joint at Kemp Little. No doubt, RAVN, Luminance, Kira Systems, and other diligence engines whose strength is in finding anomalies would respond that this is a typically sceptical response and the machine would uncover all potential anomalies and flag them for human review.

But Joint flags up the likelihood that working with a machine instead of a team of trusted associates would be a significant – and perhaps unwelcome – change for many law firm partners.

The initial challenge often arises around introducing AI in the first place. One of the major cultural challenges is convincing management and partners to find out where and how legal AI can be applied to their business. David Halliwell, director of knowledge and innovation delivery at Pinsent Masons, observes that the pressure to introduce AI often comes from clients, leading partners to ask the business support functions whether this is something the firm can deliver.

'Clients are asking the tough questions', Halliwell stated in the *Financial Times*' 'Innovative Lawyers' report. 'In the past year, we have gone from being in start-up mode to having the rest of the firm banging on our door asking about this'.[10]

Some corporations may already deploy AI, for example by using virtual assistants, chatbots, or intelligent process automation for logistics, software engineering, resourcing, financial and market analysis, and customer service. Their legal departments may utilise RAVN, Leverton, or Luminance for contract analysis and data extraction, or implement Riverview Law's Kim to manage their in-house legal function. This may lead them to ask their panel firms about their own use of AI applications, particularly when these offer the potential for faster, more cost-effective services. This is challenging, but it also represents an opportunity for law firms to collaborate with their clients on new services and resources.

The client perspective on AI will also bring fee pressures, and potentially built-in prejudices around the perceived mismatch between law and technology. Legal Zoom co-founder and chief product officer Eddie Hartman tweeted, 'If your lawyer ran discovery with a machine learning algorithm she'd written in her free time... would you trust it?' The answer would surely be that it would depend on how well it worked rather than who had written it. And Neota Logic and Riverview Law's Kim's platforms enable users to create apps and software without coding. Interestingly, nobody responded to Hartman by turning his question around and asking, 'If a technologist invented a product that handled your legal case, would you trust it?' Because the answer, clearly, is yes – DoNotPay has overturned 170,000 parking ticket cases. And that is not to mention the broad choice of case management systems, where it is unlikely that the developers were all qualified lawyers.

Because legal AI is new, and aligned with the lawtech start-up culture, it is bringing a new dynamic to legal. This is both a challenge and a fantastic opportunity. Gardner at Linklaters and Kresojevic at Freshfields found it refreshing to develop a use case for legal AI using a limited budget. 'It was like running a start-up inside a law firm', Kresojevic told the ILTA INSIGHT conference in London (held in late November 2016).

First-mover advantage

Unlike other technology, where it often pays to be a fast follower rather than a first mover and to jump in when the initial glitches and problems have been ironed out, because AI involves machine learning, being a first mover brings competitive advantage. The more work an AI system handles, the better it gets (because it applies all of its learning to every case it handles).

At Kira Systems, Waisberg highlights the danger of sitting back and waiting for others to make the first move. 'A lot of AI-powered businesses are successful because they were early adopters. It's not just about getting the technology before everyone else; the advantage is also down to what you learn from being early – taking the time to understand the system, and figure out how to work with it effectively.'

The legal AI consultancy gap

At Neota Logic, Wildisen makes the interesting observation that there is no Accenture in law. 'The big consultancy firms invest significantly in research and development (R&D) and work with clients to create solutions that they then adapt for general use, so the industry benefits from its collective experience. There is no equivalent in law, and because legal consultancies are generally smaller, they don't have the bandwidth or budgets to invest in innovation.'

RAVN's partnership with legal IT consultant Neil Cameron is a step in the right direction. Cameron works with law firms to identify and prioritise a range of opportunities using relative business impact, analysis of dependencies and integrations, and cost-benefit analysis to select the AI initiative that fits their business profile, the type of matters they handle, and their strategic objectives. Generally speaking, however, legal technology consultancies and integrators seem ill-prepared for the transformational impact of AI on the industry. As far as I am aware, there are no legal AI consultants or legal IT consultants that have significant experience with AI – and although some of the legal AI providers are former lawyers, with a couple of notable exceptions, they are generally not old enough to have spent many years working in the profession!

Consequently, innovation in legal technology, including AI, is often driven by vendors of exciting new products identifying a use case and finding a firm that is willing to develop a proof of concept – for example, legal AI first hit the mainstream when BLP and RAVN went public with LONald. The same applied to ROSS and Kira Systems.

A major challenge from the vendor perspective is the procurement process around legal and other specialist technology, as distinct from the way corporates purchase legal services. As Emilio Matthaei, CEO of Leverton, told AI Business: 'Large organisations tend to make meaningful technological decisions a lot slower than small organisations, in particular in Europe. Enterprise sales for a disruptive deep learning technology are often held back by legal departments, technology vendor reviews, and the inaccessibility of key decision makers.'[11] Leverton gets around this through integration with large distribution partners, but it remains an ongoing challenge for legal AI start-ups.

The downside of the legal AI consultancy gap is there is no obvious channel for firms to share their collective experience. The upside is that the lack of guidance from within the industry drives enterprising people in law firms – like Kresojevic and Isabel Parker, Freshfields' director of legal services innovation – to look outside legal technology, and indeed the legal sector, for new ideas. Kresojevic took the initiative to pull together the Fresh Innovate team that won the first Legal Geek hackathon,[12] and he used this experience – and validation of his efforts – to convince the firm's senior management to invest in AI. It has also led to more networking with the general AI community. Many of the leading players in legal AI attend the AI Summit and participate in other AI networks and communities, which enables them to learn from industries that are ahead of legal in terms of applying AI to their business. And as more progress is made towards a more general application of AI technology to business, legal AI will be in the vanguard.

Driving innovation

Innovation is the latest differentiator in legal technology. And AI presents a myriad of opportunities for firms that are willing to work with it. Waisberg believes that there are many areas where clients would be willing to spend more money if they could see the added value. For example, a client organisation could give all of its contract reviewing to a firm that could handle it quickly, accurately, efficiently, and cost-effectively, and the firm could make a return on that. Whereas they can now review 100 contracts, they could review 5,000 contracts and capture the value from that.

Another major challenge is the potential to increase access to affordable legal services. As Waisberg explains, this is not just about disadvantaged people – it also applies to corporates who are not getting all their legal needs met because there are no services that can deliver on their requirements in an attractive way, and at a realistic price. AI, together with the right people and processes, offers an opportunity to build new services that people will pay for.

On the other hand, innovation will continuously disrupt the legal services delivery model – and the value chain. We have covered the consequences of using machine learning to do the work that used to be handled by junior associates. The next technology potentially to disrupt legal will be blockchain. Juro CEO Richard Mabey believes that, eventually, written contracts could be surpassed by contracts written in code. Whether this happens depends on take-up, which involves an element of trust.

The challenges for legal AI involve overcoming fear and building trust. As Futures Laboratory CEO Trevor Hardy said at the Global Futures Forum, held in New York in October 2016, 'innovation is not just about technology; it is about reinventing trust'. And, ultimately, the incursion of AI into legal will relate to how far we are prepared to trust a 'robot lawyer'.

Technology will continue to change and have an impact on our lives in different ways, and AI is already finding a place in a variety of legal services provision – but law is ultimately a people business. While legal AI is supporting the business of law by speeding up due diligence and contract comparison, as well as simplifying and expediting litigation support and building efficiencies in to professional and business support functions, it is also maintaining the position of the law and the legal sector as a pillar of society by upholding people's ability to exercise and defend their legal rights and extending access to justice. One of the biggest advantages of AI-powered applications is that, because they are infinitely scalable, once trust has been established, the momentum increases rapidly and exponentially. The following chapters look ahead at the potential for legal AI to transform the industry.

References
1. Robot-lawyers.com.au.
2. For more on the ABA Commission on the Future of Legal Services, see: www.americanbar.org/groups/centers_commissions/commission-on-the-future-of-legal-services.html.
3. 'RAVN Systems releases RAVN ACE for automated data extraction of ISDA documents using Artificial Intelligence', in RAVN's

quarterly newsletter, February 2016. Available at: www.ravn.co.uk/ravn-systems-releases-ravn-ace-automated-data-extraction-isda-documents-using-artificial-intelligence.

4. 'AI start-up "Legit" to disrupt patent world, secures seedcamp funding', *Artificial Lawyer*, 25 November, 2016. Available at: artificiallawyer.com/2016/11/25/ai-start-up-legit-to-disrupt-patent-world-secures-seedcamp-funding/.

5. Rosenbaum, E. 'Can elite law firms survive the rise of artificial intelligence? The jury is still out', CNBC website, 17 November 2016. Available at: www.cnbc.com/2016/11/17/can-cash-cow-of-elite-legal-firms-survive-ai-the-jury-is-still-out.html.

6. Dipshan, R., 'As AI portends the death of the billable hour, law firms face new reality', *Legaltech News*, 23 November 2016. Available at: www.legaltechnews.com/id=1202773158485/As-AI-Portends-the-Death-of-the-Billable-Hour-Law-Firms-Face-New-Reality?cmp=share_twitter.

7. Wells, M. 'What AI is really going to do to the legal industry', LinkedIn post, 22 November 2016. Available at: www.linkedin.com/pulse/what-ai-really-going-do-legal-industry-martyn-wells?trk=pulse_spock-articles.

8. 'Legal engineering – A dictionary definition', *Wavelength Law Blog*, 8 November 2016. Available at: www.wavelength.law/blog/2016/11/8/legal-engineering-a-dictionary-definition.

9. 'Are you a legal engineer', *Wavelength Law Blog*, 29 August 2016. Available at: www.wavelength.law/blog/2016/8/29/are-you-a-legal-engineer.

10. Croft, J. 'Artificial intelligence disrupting the business of law', *Financial Times*, 6 October 2016. Available at: www.ft.com/content/5d96dd72-83eb-11e6-8897-2359a58ac7a5.

11. AI Business, 'Leverton enabling "more educated, faster and better decision-making" says CEO Emilio Matthaei', 5 September 2016. Available at: aibusiness.org/leverton-enabling-more-educated-faster-and-better-decision-making-says-ceo-emilio-matthaei/#sthash.fvT7J6JY.dpuf.

12. Disclaimer: I was one of the judges, but at the time I had not encountered any of the team!

Part 4:
Looking ahead…
but not too far!

Chapter 9:
Legal AI – Creating the future

'The best way to predict the future is to create it', said Abraham Lincoln. This chapter takes a futurist perspective on the likely impact of legal AI on legal services delivery, which will depend on the speed of take-up and the level of enthusiasm among lawyers and legal services providers. I consulted futurists and AI experts who are closely associated with the legal sector, but who also interact with other industry verticals, some of which have been (retail) or are about to be (public transportation) transformed beyond recognition by AI. All of the contributors speak and write extensively about legal AI, but they are not practising lawyers or part of the legal establishment. Legal futurist Chrissie Lightfoot, global futurist and strategist Rohit Talwar, and Robert Woolliams, editor and online community manager at AI Business, highlight some of the issues related to and influences on where legal AI is going next and encourage lawyers, legal services providers – and technologists – to engage in creating the future of law by embracing AI and other emerging technologies.

Can AI drive client centricity?
Chrissie Lightfoot is an entrepreneur, lawyer, legal futurist, and consultant who advises the global legal sector. She is CEO of EntrepreneurLawyer Limited, a global consulting business specialising in the future of legal services, artificial intelligence, and robotics in the law; relationship 'SocialHuman' sales; and personal branding. As CEO of AI Tech Support Ltd, Chrissie is the creator of AI lawyer LISA. She is also a futurist, writer, international keynote speaker, legal and business commentator, and solicitor (non-practising). She is the author of two books: *The Naked Lawyer* and *Tomorrow's Naked Lawyer.*

My observation and experience to date is that lawyers and traditional law firms are obsessed with how AI and robots will impact lawyers: our roles, firms, business models, and futures. But the vast majority of practising lawyers, when considering take-up and deployment of AI, and robots in particular, hold a biased lawyer-centric perspective, and are stifled by legacy structures and governance, and outdated operational practices.

For example, reports made in October 2016 of Howard Kennedy's lawyers being locked out of their computers for failing to clock up 5.6 billable hours a day, reveals something rather alarming: those most affected by a penalty system designed to shame partners and junior solicitors by withdrawing access to the firm's technology will be the law firm's clients.

Lawyers and businesses of law ought to be preoccupied with how the positive use of (or choice not to deploy) AI technology will impact existing clients, new clients, and potential clients – the latent legal market. After all, no clients means no job, career, company, or future!

What if we traded our lawyer-centric perspective for a client-centric one? We have been asking: Can computers be lawyers? Can computers do what lawyers do? Will lawyers be replaced? Are lawyers being replaced? Should lawyers be replaced? Is this the end of lawyers? These questions presume that lawyers do the right things, and do them well, in every legal situation. The truth is, we do not.

The focus of those kinds of questions is on how, whether, and when AI will do those same things. The problem with this lawyer-centric perspective is that legal services exist for clients, not lawyers. If this mantra seems suspect to you, ask yourself:

- Do transportation services exist for the drivers – or for you, the rider?
- Do medical services exist for the doctors – or for you, the patient?
- Do educational services exist for the teachers – or for you and your kids to learn?
- Accordingly, does legal AI exist for the lawyer – or for the client?

Today, cognitive computing, AI, and robots (automation and algorithmic software) are currently (and mainly) used, and being considered for use, in the legal ecosystem in a lawyer-centric way – as a carthorse rather than a racehorse... or a unicorn. That is, they are currently augmenting legal services delivery behind the scenes within law firms. Lawyers are primarily using AI technology such as IBM Watson, ROSS, RAVN, KIRA, Luminance, Neota Logic, and others to benefit themselves, to streamline and improve business and/or fee-earning processes – that is, to bring increased efficiency within existing business models.

Until recently, firms like BakerHostetler, BLP, Travers Smith, Linklaters, Deloitte, Clifford Chance, DLA Piper, Freshfields Bruckhaus Deringer, Slaughter & May (to name a few) have deployed legal AI in a lawyer-centric way, which means that the benefit does not always filter down to the client. The tech is deployed in some aspects of work that the firm has not previously charged for, but where they will now be making significant resource and time savings for both the lawyer/law firm and client.

In essence, legal AI is being used by law firms primarily to defend their existing business models, and not as a creative disrupter to bring radical change that includes extending legal services provision to a previously unserved and untapped market. Legal AI provides the opportunity to lucratively rethink and reinvent legal services offerings. A shift of mindset and switch of focus is required by lawyers and law firms to exploit the greatest benefit that AI and machine learning technology bring to the legal industry; they provide cost-effective, scalable solutions. AI allows the creation, delivery, and exploitation of new legal services (by all kinds of legal services providers), never before possible, that can now be made more widely available to the many, rather than the few. This is where I see the near future of legal AI.

The legal profession has enjoyed a monopoly for 800 years by locking up knowledge, experience, and intelligence in the individual lawyer's brain. But no more. Now, with emerging technologies that will continue to infiltrate the legal ecosystem, a lawyer's savvy and nous can be captured, harvested, exploited, and scaled – whether that lawyer is working in a Magic Circle firm or as a one-man wonder, or whether that lawyer is a human or a robot.

Let's not ignore the fact that the millennial generation (the legal buyer of today and tomorrow) has already taken to robo-advisors. For example, the 2016 investor satisfaction survey reveals robo-advisors appeal most to millennial investors. 66 per cent of Canadians born after 1982 indicated that they would be interested in robo-advice if their financial services provider were to offer it, compared to 54 per cent of all investors. As in the financial world, so in the legal world. There's a reason Deloitte et al have embraced legal AI.

I predict that BigLaw and Magic Circle firms will continue with the aggressive take-up of legal AI and focus on utilising the technology to harvest and exploit the knowledge, experience, and intelligence of their lawyers across the globe – currently locked in legacy (and today's) documents and data within their ivory towers – to create overall value in, and for, the law firm entity. Some of this will filter down to the firms' blue-chip clients.

However, I also predict a new wave of businesses and/or entrepreneurial lawyers within existing law firms will rise up, along with a whole range of 'robot lawyer' products and services, to begin serving the 'unmet need' of the masses that I, Lord Faulkner, and many others have spoken about in the past.

In spite of the regulatory issues and 'access to data' problems inherent in some uses of legal AI that will need to be addressed before legal AI can truly take-off in jurisdictions across the world, I am confident that within two years legal AI will be truly mainstream in the UK legal industry; across most types, sizes, and sectors of legal services provider; and touching the majority of areas of law, consumer and business.

Ultimately, I predict that legal AI and robot lawyers have the potential to reach and will begin to serve those people, businesses, societies, and economies that need AI legal services the most; that is, the growing backbone of a global society made up of consumers such as you and me. The drive for this will come from millennials, entrepreneurs, and small businesses – people who are striving to make a living in a digital world where, within ten years, as many as 40–60 per cent of blue-collar and white-collar workers' jobs across the globe may have been replaced by a robot. If ever there was a time to be entrepreneurial, it is now. If ever there was a time for legal AI to help entrepreneurs and small and medium-sized enterprises (SMEs), it is now.

In the UK the great 'legally unwashed' comprises 54 per cent of all SMEs, and some reports reveal as many as four in five businesspeople. According to the American Bar Association, one in three US consumers 'muddle through' rather than consulting a lawyer because of barriers to entry, which include price/cost, lack of time or availability, inconvenience, fear of talking with a (human) lawyer who appears intellectually superior, the incomprehensibility of legal language (legalese and other language issues) and legal complexity, and/or a desire to do some of the legal work for themselves.

The take-up of legal AI, robot automation, and robot lawyering in existing law firms has already begun to be client driven, and I predict that this will continue with increasing market pressure over the next two years. Legal AI and robot lawyering will be deployed by smart providers such as new legal tech companies, spin-off boutique legal services providers, individual entrepreneurial lawyers (within and outside traditional firms), and/or virtual lawyers providing differentiated and bespoke forms of robot lawyering (such as algorithmic law) direct to the legal buyer – both consumers and businesses.

It won't be about robots versus lawyers battling it out for the human lawyer's job. It won't be about robot lawyers supporting human lawyers. It won't even be about robot lawyers replacing human lawyers. This is inevitable. It's already begun. And within five to ten years AI won't even need to be supervised.

It is, and will be, about robot lawyers continuing to support and replace human lawyers. That's okay. There will be new roles for the smart lawyers of today, tomorrow. If you realise, appreciate, and accept that AI is currently – and will in the future be – about placing robot automation and robot lawyers (the human lawyer's brain) where they aren't now (but ought to be), you need not fear the robot lawyer and/or legal AI. You should welcome it as a magical opportunity to serve a great unmet need. If you don't, a competitor will.

Unleashing the true potential of AI – Building the exponential law firm

Rohit Talwar is a global futurist and strategist, and founder of Fast Future Research. He works with global businesses to create the future, helping them understand how mega trends, emerging ideas, new business models, and disruptive developments in science and technology could impact individuals, society, business, industries, and government. He leads studies on transformative drivers of change for the next decade, science and technology developments over the next 40 years, impacts of emerging technologies on the legal sector, human enhancement, and the shadow economy. He has authored *Designing Your Future: Key Trends, Challenges and Choices*, and edited *Achieving Transformation and Renewal in Financial Services*.

The article below formed the basis of Rohit Talwar's presentation at ILTA INISIGHT in London, in November 2016.

Artificial intelligence represents both the biggest opportunity and potentially the greatest threat to the legal profession since its formation. This is part of a bigger global revolution – where society, business, and government are likely to experience more change in the next 20–30 years than in the last 500. This large-scale disruption is being driven by the combined effects of AI and a range of other disruptive technologies whose speed, power, and capability are growing at an exponential rate or faster – and which both enable AI and are fed by it.

These include quantum computing, blockchain technology, the internet of things (IoT), big data, cloud services, smart cities, and human augmentation – all of which could literally be hundreds or thousands of times more powerful and impactful within a decade. The resulting changes will lead to the total transformation of every business sector; the birth of new trillion-dollar industries; and a complete rethink of the law, regulation, legal infrastructures, and the supporting governance systems for literally every activity on the planet.

At present, the sheer scale of the opportunity is lost on all but a few genuinely forward-thinking players across the legal ecosystem. The majority in the sector are either blissfully unaware of what impact AI could have or they are becoming obsessed with the internal applications of AI. In many cases, a natural tendency towards risk aversion is leaving firms paralysed by fears of declining revenues, commoditisation, the depersonalisation of the sector, and the loss of professional roles. These fears have in turn driven reluctance to even understand, let alone embrace, the true opportunities presented by AI and its disruptive technology cousins.

I believe law firms can and should escape from conventional wisdom and look to drive exponential improvements in internal performance and market growth by exploiting the opportunities presented by AI and other emerging technologies. Indeed, some in the legal sector are already diving deep to understand what they are and their true commercial potential. However, many are still more worried about the potential negative impacts of AI on the $650-billion legal services market, and are proceeding cautiously as a result. I would argue that the real exponential growth opportunity lies in helping the world respond to the transformative impact of AI on the roughly $78-trillion global economy.

Driving internal transformation

The pace of AI development is stunning – even to those working in the sector. Indeed, the resounding victory of Google DeepMind's AlphaGo over the world Go champion in March 2016 demonstrated just how far machine learning has evolved. AlphaGo was equipped with a sophisticated learning algorithm that allowed it to deduce the rules and possible moves from observing thousands of games. AI has truly transformative potential – with a wide range of legal applications emerging, such as:

- Predicting the likely outcome of a case;
- Determining the best structure for a contract;
- Suggesting how best to approach a new matter; or
- Making sense of literally billions of data points across the web to spot new and emerging risks and legal threats.

I envisage five broad categories where we will see increasing use of AI within law firms in the next three to five years:

- Automation of legal tasks and processes;
- Decision support and outcome prediction;
- Creation of new product and service offerings;
- Process design and matter management; and
- Practice management.

In addition, we are likely to see the growing use of AI both by in-house legal teams and in a range of online platforms offering direct services to businesses and individuals. AI will also power developments using blockchain technology (the secure transaction encoding mechanisms that underpin most digital currencies such as Bitcoin). For example:

- Smart contracts encoded in software which require no human intervention;

- Distributed autonomous organisations (DAOs) with no human employees that exist entirely in software;

- Decentralised arbitration and mediation networks – which effectively operate as 'opt-in' global justice systems for commercial transactions, and which sit outside the existing national and global mechanisms;

- Algocracy (algorithmic democracy) – creating global codes of legal transactions by codifying and automating legal documents, including contracts, permits, organisational documents, and consents; and

- Rewriting and embedding the law in software – e.g. automatic fines, drawing evidence from the IoT, standardised open-source legal documents, and automated judgements.

So how might AI evolve within the sector?

Here is a plausible timeline of AI developments in the legal sector over the next five years:

The next 18 months

- Increase in law firms establishing internal technology innovation labs, creating seed funds to invest in legal technology start-ups, and running joint experiments with technology providers and clients;

- A number of firms and in-house teams will run AI trials and develop applications that create smarter internal processes;

- A range of trials and applications of AI for lawyer decision support;
- Launch of the first client-facing AI applications and new AI-enabled products and services;
- Growth of FinTech – rising pressure from financial services to embrace AI/ blockchain technology – with legal cost reduction a key driver; and
- The emergence of blockchain smart contracts and DAOs.

The next three years

- Clear evidence of lawyer replacement by smart technologies;
- Widespread and accelerating deployment of AI on core law firm processes;
- Meaningful penetration of AI into in-house legal;
- First truly AI-centric law firms;
- Significant range of AI-based solutions offered direct to consumers and SMEs and technology businesses; and
- Widespread adoption of blockhain smart contracts in newer firms and the rise of DAOs in both the private and public sectors.

The next five years

- Applications starting to emerge that display near-human levels of intelligence (artificial general intelligence) in certain domains;
- First examples of true Algocracy – countries moving to digitising, automating, and embedding the law;

- Blockchain, smart contracts, and DAOs in widespread use in financial services and other sectors;

- 20–50 per cent of 'routine' legal work by sector fully automated by clients with no law firm involvement;

- New technology-centric legal sector entrants from the last five years competing head on with BigLaw; and

- AI will be in widespread use across law firms and frequently mandated by clients.

Going for the bigger prize

While AI can clearly be disruptive within law firms, the real AI transformation opportunity lies in the broader marketplace. Indeed, by focusing almost exclusively on the internal impact on the approximately $650-billion legal services market, the sector is missing the point. I believe that AI – combined with the other disruptive technologies mentioned – could redefine every existing business sector and drive the creation of new ones – leading to dramatic growth of the global economy to $120 billion or more in the next decade.

AI and the technologies it enables such as robotics, blockchain, Medtech, Edtech, and FinTech will drive the reinvention of existing sectors from media, healthcare, education, and transport to retail, construction, and financial services. AI is already enabling the next wave of trillion-dollar sectors and developments such as autonomous vehicles, DAOs, synthetic biology, smart materials, intelligent cities, blockchain data networks, and smart contracts. AI is also driving interest in new economic paradigms, new notions of money, and new legal models such as Algocracy.

All of these developments will require the interpretation, reframing, and redrafting of legal frameworks; and the creation of new legal concepts and dispute resolution mechanisms to encompass new political, economic, social, and business paradigms. So, while AI will undoubtedly have a transformative impact on how law firms work internally, the true exponential growth opportunity lies in helping governments, businesses, and civil society to understand, regulate for, and adjust to the coming waves of AI-enabled disruption.

Here are a few examples of those new legal sector opportunities:

- Establishing the governing principles and regulations around the use and insurance of self-driving vehicles;

- Rollback, recovery, contract review, and dispute arbitration for fully automated, blockchain-based financial transaction systems;

- Governance and 'right of redress' protocols where AI systems are replacing human decision makers in areas as diverse as healthcare, social security, and legal dispute resolution;

- Usage control and privacy protection within the AI systems that will manage and interpret the massive data flows arising from the IoT;

- Creating regulatory frameworks to govern the conduct of and dispute resolution for DAOs; and

- Determining governance and monitoring frameworks for scientific research which is designed and conducted entirely by AI systems, e.g. the creation of new lifeforms.

Over the next five to ten years we will see these and many more opportunities start to emerge as existing sectors are transformed, and new ones emerge. AI and the related technologies will enable the creation of entirely new markets, commercial concepts, business models, and delivery mechanisms – ideas we couldn't even begin to imagine or describe today. For forward-thinking law firms, these developments offer the potential to drive exponential growth in revenues – if we give ourselves permission to invest the time in understanding the brave new world technologies and their transformative potential. Whether firms seize the opportunity or become paralysed by fear and indecision will ultimately be a matter of choice and a function of our willingness to step into the unknown and start learning.

A global perspective on legal AI

AI Business is a leading media and events organisation focused on the practical application of AI in the business world, and organiser of the AI Summit series of international conferences. Robert Woolliams, editor and online community manager, who is in constant contact with AI business leaders from all over the world, brings a broader perspective to the future direction of legal AI.

In the last 18 months, it has become clear that AI has the potential to have a profound and transformative impact on the professional services industries. AI Business predicts that in the next 18 months, and in the years to follow, we will see unparalleled efficiency and productivity in law and professional services generally, due to the advancement and implementation of artificially intelligent technologies.

Although the UK and US have seen the greatest uptake of legal AI applications, with the UK's RAVN Systems working with UK and European firms, ROSS Intelligence gaining a strong foothold in US firms, and Kira Systems winning business from Magic Circle, BigLaw, and other international firms. America's largest law firm by revenue, Latham & Watkins, is test-driving new IBM Watson-based applications, including cognitive and predictive coding technologies. In the professional services realm, Deloitte has partnered with IPsoft and their cognitive IT solutions. AI technology supporting corporate legal departments is fast becoming a global phenomenon, with use cases appearing across Europe – Leverton is based in Berlin and operates across multiple languages and jurisdictions, and Riverview Law's Kim is available in English and Spanish.

Even in firms that are not yet at the point of application, the conversations are happening, and the industry's biggest players are waking up to the realisation that AI is becoming an essential consideration for those looking to stay ahead of the competition – not only does it maximise return on investment of time and resources, it also brings greater accuracy and eliminates human error from the work carried out. These benefits, is it also important to note, do not come at the expense of hundreds and thousands of paralegal roles and a dearth of opportunities for the law graduates of tomorrow; instead, AI will open up paralegals and trainees to more creative, hands-on tasks that their academic hard work has prepared them for. This is a hugely promising start, particularly when we remember that this is a field that is traditionally very resistant to change, not least when it comes to technology.

Investments in AI by law firms will only become more frequent, with increasing financial backing and a greater level of internal strategic thought required. AI in the legal sector is set to disrupt clerical tasks and indications are that investment in legal AI will rise above $55 million over the next eight years. Moreover, this trend will spread across Europe and Asia as more use cases are established and technologies become more reliable, accessible, and cost-effective.

The technology is currently limited to handling particular tasks – research or contract analysis, for instance – at the firms that have so far applied it, but soon these technologies will become the de facto way of handling particular tasks at all firms. And as various forms of AI improve in accuracy and decrease in price, more and more firms will begin to access and experiment with it. Imagine the potential of deep-learning-powered image recognition in criminal law, for instance, or the benefits that refined NLP systems could bring to the relationship between lawyer and machine.

Once accepted into the mainstream, AI will transform the processes of entire legal departments, where the technology is already going beyond information extraction to predict outcomes – for instance in insurance, where systems such as those deployed at Bradford & Barthel in the US and Hodge Jones & Allen in the UK assess whether or not it is worth pursuing a personal injury claim. In the future, RAVN CTO Jan Van Hoecke suggests this could extend to court rulings at the top level. 'AI can consider a lot more information than humans – if the pattern is in the data, AI can probably predict it. The question is: do you have the right data, and are the parameters correct?'

He is not alone in his conviction that, as long as the quality of data allows it, the ability of AI to predict is potentially limitless.

Chapter 10:
Robot lawyers – A new chapter in legal IT

Legal AI has been described as heralding a 'new chapter' in the legal technology arms race. It will surely replace some roles and create others, and it is already altering legal technology purchasing patterns. This chapter speculates on some of the influencing factors on the future direction of legal AI.

Progress so far indicates that the current application of legal AI could well be part of an evolution that will be a game changer for legal services, not because it will change the basic premise of what lawyers do – or replace them all – but because it will create shifts in the value chain, and therefore change the legal business model in terms of legal services procurement, billing – and margins. Making legal AI work effectively will also require a culture shift that is already happening. But there is clearly some way to go. This chapter looks at the changing perception of legal AI from something that threatens the industry to a catalyst for transformation, innovation, and opportunity.

While I have been working on this book, there have been multiple new entrants into the legal AI market, along with a sea change in the profession's approach to AI. In just under a year, it has moved from fear that robots will replace lawyers to general acceptance that legal AI is here to stay – and is certainly part of the future. The chief executive of the Law Society of England and Wales urged the profession to embrace machine learning and artificial intelligence and build on it to deliver better services. The Law Society also sponsored the Legal Geek lawtech start-up conference in London. Magic Circle and BigLaw firms as well as established legal technology vendors are investing time and resources in partnering with AI suppliers and experts to develop and implement AI-powered technology. Although, at the time of publication, there are no dedicated legal AI consultants, established legal IT consultant Neil Cameron (whose clients include more than half of the top 50 law firms in the UK among others across the globe) is now working in partnership with RAVN to develop use cases for legal AI, and to advise law firms on how AI can fit into their business. Pay-as-you-go legal AI offerings are making the technology accessible to the wider legal services market too.

To some extent, 'robots' in the form of intelligent automation are already replacing lawyers in some discrete elements of legal services, and so far, this is generally considered to be a good thing with AI bringing reliable, scalable, faster services to more people, increasing commercial benefits, and broadening access to justice. From the lawyers' perspective, AI is augmenting their efforts rather than replacing them and freeing them up from essential, but repetitive, tasks to do more (interesting and value-added) work.

The big question remains whether AI will eventually mean less work for lawyers, and therefore a need for fewer (human) lawyers. How will it transform legal services delivery – and legal services themselves? As outlined in Chapter 7, Kira Systems' Noah Waisberg believes that, rather than taking lawyers' jobs, AI-powered legal applications will create *more* work for lawyers as clients are more likely to utilise services that are delivered quickly, efficiently, and cost-effectively.

On the other hand, futurist Rohit Talwar (featured in the previous chapter) has identified multiple ways in which he believes smart technology will replace lawyers in their current roles. But it will also create new markets for legal services, and new roles. Most of Talwar's predictions for the next 18 months are already happening, although so far there are no indications that the developments he highlights are leading to lawyers being replaced. Below, I examine some of his predictions for the next year and a half:

1. *Increase in law firms establishing internal technology inno-vation labs, creating seed funds to invest in legal technology start-ups, and running joint experiments with technology providers and clients.*

    Dentons NextLaw Labs and ROSS, Clifford Chance and Kira Systems/Neota Logic, and BLP and RAVN's LONald are all examples of law firms funding and collaborating with start-ups and working on legal use cases with AI vendors, but none of this means replacing lawyers – in fact, this type of research requires lawyer involvement.

2. *A number of firms and in-house teams will run AI trials and develop applications that create smarter internal processes.*

    Pinsent Masons, Linklaters, and Deloitte are all doing this, but smarter internal processes are not replacing lawyers; rather they are redeploying them to other work.

3. *We will see a range of trials and applications of AI for lawyer decision support.*

    Bradford & Barthel's Spherical Models, Premonition, and LexisNexis' Lex Machina are all examples. This is about using big data analytics to support strategic and prac-tical decision making – strategic decision making around whether to pursue a case; operational decision making around which counsel to appoint for a particular case.

4. *Launch of the first client-facing AI applications and new AI-enabled products and services.*

    Taylor Wessing and other firms have built apps on the Neota Logic platform, but these client-facing resources complement rather than replace legal services. For example, supporting compliance by enabling clients to check whether they will be affected by legislative and regulatory changes, and therefore need to seek legal advice. Another example is information architect Ben Gardner and his team at Linklaters using open-source software to create an automated name-checking system that conforms to banking regulations.

5. *Growth of FinTech and rising pressure from financial services to embrace AI.*

    This may be a key influencer explaining why legal AI adoption has started in transactional work. Legal AI vendors such as RAVN also work with the banking and financial sector and firms including Clifford Chance and Linklaters introduced AI into their banking and capital markets teams first.

6. *Emergence of blockchain smart contracts and DAOs.*

    This is not strictly legal AI, but again it is a key influence on its direction and is a developing source of legal work.

Chrissie Lightfoot (featured in the previous chapter) also sees legal AI creating opportunities for new services and opening up latent markets. She envisages legal AI helping law firms to become more genuinely client-centric, developing the concept of AI connecting us with our humanity, as well as bringing efficiency and scalability. This is already happening. From the technology perspective, firms are introducing AI-powered client-facing applications that make their expertise and advice available in a tailored way to multiple clients simultaneously. AI enables firms to introduce applications in response to legislative and regulatory changes – and advise on the implications of political decisions like Brexit and the 2016 US presidential election.

From a practical perspective, firms that utilise AI to augment their lawyers – for example, with instant document searches, due diligence, the ability to extract and reuse information from documents and precedents, and handle repetitive tasks accurately and instantaneously – are freeing up their lawyers to focus more time and energy on understanding their clients' position and business needs, and to work on strategies, negotiations, and other human concerns. Law and business are, ultimately, human endeavours and client engagement along with a personalised service are what differentiate one excellent firm from another.

At AI Business, Robert Woolliams (also featured in Chapter 9) is more focused on the short-term, and envisages legal AI take-up being driven by market forces – i.e. clients will choose the firms that utilise AI resources to provide efficient, cost-effective, and scalable services, and those that do not will be unable to compete. As AI supports competitive advantage in legal as in other industry verticals, it will become the de facto platform for service delivery. There is also an opportunity for AI-powered collaboration with clients, as is demonstrated by the partnership between RAVN, Neota Logic, and HighQ. As the legal sector continues to catch up with industries that are ahead in terms of AI adoption, technological developments will no doubt present more opportunities for law firms to learn from and collaborate with clients and experts in other sectors, perhaps finding new ways to close the legal AI consultancy gap.

Beyond the hype – Transforming, but not taking over

Leading US legal consultant Ron Friedmann posted a video on Twitter wondering why there has been so much media hype surrounding legal AI. He used this as the basis for a blog post on AI's potential impact on the practice of law.[1]

'I don't recall there being nearly as much excitement about three developments: PCs, the internet, and social media. There weren't a lot of commentators or practicing lawyers saying any of those things would change everything', he said. 'AI has a lot of promise, but to date its application has been limited to e-discovery, document automation, and due diligence for deals. Even in those areas it's not clear that the employment impact has been huge or that it changes dramatically how lawyers practice day to day. Maybe I'm missing something and in the future AI will dramatically change the legal market.'

My response is that legal AI media hype has arisen due to a combination of factors. Legal AI is an immature market. We didn't think the internet would change everything – but it did. And one of the things it changed was the number of media platforms and the way we consume media. We are living in a post-PC, post-internet era and social media is part of our communications landscape. We are also living in the age of media hype. And because we've experienced relatively recently technologies that have changed the way we live and work, we are looking for the 'next big thing'. On top of this, AI and robots are scary and exciting in a way that PCs or the internet were not, because they emulate human complexity. AI sparks our imagination as it is the stuff of science fiction to have robots that do things for us – and potentially replace people or become a danger to humanity! The excitement and media hype that surrounds AI is exacerbated by world-class scientific thinkers and innovators Stephen Hawking and Elon Musk warning that AI will ultimately kill off the human race. But they were not referring to legal AI!

I agree with Friedmann that, so far, legal AI isn't living up to its hype. Lawyers are not about to be replaced by an e-discovery system, a due diligence engine, or even a legal chatbot. The hype is contextual as there's a buzz around technology generally as a game-changer. However, like the other technologies Friedmann mentions, as take-up spreads across the industry and legal AI becomes more prevalent, it will help to establish a new legal technology landscape.

Ryan McClead, vice president of client engagement and strategy at Neota Logic, wrote a blog post in response to Friedmann, saying that hype around AI was more about how we define it than what we can do with it, citing Google, Siri, and Alexa as AI we take for granted.[2] 'The more we see of it, the less we believe it to truly represent artificial intelligence. AI is always just beyond the horizon. Just on the other side of the next technological breakthrough. It's always something just slightly better than what we can do right now', he wrote, reflecting to some extent legal academic Paresh Kathrani's sentiment that many of the ethical and regulatory issues around legal AI are ontological rather than practical – i.e. they are to do with classification rather than application.

This book has shown that legal AI is already here and that it is a game-changer. But it may take longer than we anticipate to live up to expectations. This is in part because technology take-up is often imperceptible until it reaches a tipping point, and legal AI is not there yet.

Martin Joseph Brej, vice president of global services at Thomson Reuters Elite, offers a pragmatic perspective. 'AI – in legal at least – is following the conventional technology maturity curve. It's finding simple, specific point solutions and use cases before moving to a more generalisable capability. Conversational AI will come to legal via legal knowledge assistants like ROSS and via generalised virtual assistants.'

Brej sees legal AI as a gateway technology to the generalised AI that the Partnership on AI and others are anticipating. 'Before we get truly generalised AI, we will see applications that are tuned and tailored to specific business verticals. For example, a legal services bot could be trained to understand billing and costs or to direct its focus on a certain matter or type of matter. Conversational legal AI will come too, but it's taking a while', he adds.

Brej offers other observations around what will be the next legal AI milestone when the chasm is crossed from early adoption to mass market take-up. 'Technology develops those capabilities but strategic choices need to be made in order to reach the target market. What we're seeing in legal AI is people finding sweet spots where they are making technical capability relevant, appealing, and useable. The next phase involves identifying the right place to cross the chasm. We are already seeing many companies offering similar capabilities, and the ones who become successful are those who figure out how to cross the chasm and get their stuff out into the mass market. How long it will take to do that is anyone's guess.'

As various sections of this book have highlighted, AI has the potential to create new legal services and new legal technology offerings. However, technologists at IBM Watson, for example, are not necessarily familiar with the industry verticals that use their platforms, so one way of broadening their reach is to open up the technology to other developers. Brej explains: 'One way for platform developers like IBM Watson to find multiple ways of crossing the chasm is to OEM[3] the technology and enable specialist developers who have insights into industry problems to be solved to take the technology forward. Specific use cases are the near-term sweet spots for legal AI. One way for vendors to access these is to open up their technology for others to use to identify new use cases and guide them to where their technology can cross the chasm. APIs[4] are one way of doing that.'

For example, Thomson Reuters Elite is developing Amazon Alexa skills so that lawyers and others can access the Elite solutions via an Amazon Echo device. 'Because Amazon is opening up Alexa's general conversational ability to Thomson Reuters and other developers, its use is likely to start moving from homes to offices', explains Brej. 'So, Amazon's skills strategy allows other developers to broaden Alexa's use and help the platform flourish.'

Tom Wilson of Seedcamp agrees: 'Legal AI is not holistic – yet. It's all narrow. But its narrow applications are gradually making legal AI more accessible.'

To reiterate a point made in Chapter 8, law firms are notoriously slow to adopt new technology. But when they do, they do it wholesale. For legal AI to be genuinely transformational, the legal industry will require another culture change – to a more collaborative approach. My prediction is that this won't take as long as most commentators imagine – because AI is already changing the legal sector. The challenges that arise because AI is a relatively unknown quantity in legal mean that the established providers and consultants were not part of the first wave and are only now finding ways to work with it, which they have to do to keep up with dynamic new entrants into the legal and legal technology space. Because, with some exceptions, there are not a lot of AI experts in legal, law firms and legal IT vendors need to collaborate with specialist AI providers, who equally tend to have limited experience in the legal sector, to create brand new AI-powered solutions for legal-specific services. Neota Logic and RAVN have been particularly active in the collaboration space.

It is likely that as AI becomes more accessible and affordable, it will become the de facto platform for some legal services and resources in the same way that cloud computing is now. Moreover, rather than replacing lawyers, an AI-first approach will expand the legal services market in new directions.

Kathrani sees law and AI evolving together. 'There is a tendency to look at law and AI as a dichotomy, but it is not a binary relationship. It is more like yin and yang. As one changes, the other evolves too. Law is evolving as everything around it evolves and the practice of law needs to evolve too. AI is not about to replace lawyers, but the practice of law will evolve and adapt. Law and lawyers will remain relevant because law is a lived experience. The question is how they remain relevant, and AI will surely influence that.'

Legal AI is developing fast and, beyond the hype, it is changing the industry in an irreversible way. This book has plotted its progression and some of its dimensions, and perhaps has indicated the way forward, but although it includes valuable input from legal futurists, it is not futurism. You could say it is now-ism. As William Gibson wrote, 'The future is already here, it is just not evenly distributed'.

References

1. Friedman, R. 'Artificial Intelligence (AI) in legal – Why the hype?', 22 Novmber 2016. Available at: Prismlegal.com/artificial-intelligence-ai-in-legal-why-the-hype/.
2. McClead, R., 'Why all the AI hype in legal? – A response to Ron Friedmann', *3 Geeks and a Law Blog*, 21 November 2016. Available at: www.geeklawblog.com/2016/11/why-all-ai-hype-in-legal-response-to.html.
3. An original equipment manufacturer (OEM) is a company that makes a part or subsystem that is used in another company's end product – for

example a company that makes wires which are used in a machine made by a second company.
4. An application programming interface (API) is a set of routines, protocols, and tools for building software applications. These are the building blocks for a computer programme that are then assembled by a developer.

Index